The
MERCHANDIZING
of the Almighty in the
AMERICAN
CHURCH

Is a critique of the American church and it's decline

By

DR. DORSETT D. SMITH

PROMINENT
BOOKS
EDGE

5830 E 2nd St, Ste 7000 #9983
Casper, WY 82609
USA

Dedicated to my beloved wife Dottie and friends, but most of all to Martai Wheeling for the constant encouragement and accountability that was so greatly needed and appreciated.

CONTENTS

INTRODUCTION

I have felt led to share my insights about the contemporary American church. The old saying is "when America sneezes, the world catches a cold." The influence of the American church is very profound. Many Christians in the Third World imitate the American model of Church practice. It is to my brothers and sisters in the Third World nations that I dedicate this book. It is written as a warning about the increasingly pagan and heretical nature of the American church. It is based on a series of nocturnal awakenings around 3:30 a.m. in the summer of 2007. I received a series of dreams or visions over several months of cruise ships, each one representing a humorous characterization of some of the extremes found in different facets of the American church. Often in scripture boats or ships are metaphors for the church and the sea is used as a metaphor for unsaved nations and people groups. (Jonah 1:3-17, Matthew 8:23-27, Mark 4:35-41, Luke 8:22-25) I wrote my thoughts down in my journal and after many months and the urging of friends, I decided to put them in a book.

This book is primarily an allegory and in a progressive fashion answers the question: "what is the true versus the false Gospel?" Each chapter is a theological treatise in itself. The book is best read slowly, one chapter at a time, and pondered and digested before proceeding to the next chapter, which will discuss an entirely different topic of biblical theology. I can only treat a variety of theological concepts superficially. My purpose is to inspire the reader to find other resources that explain various concepts. I am a fallen human being saved by grace who makes absolutely no claim on perfect revelation from God or some type of super-spirituality. However, I don't think it was too much pizza for dinner that awoke me in the middle of the night with these visions and dreams. I only can offer humbly what I heard and have seen in the spirit world. Use discernment about what you read. Chew on the meat and spit out the bones! I think the reader will find something in this book from the Lord that will speak to him or her; (just ignore what is from my flesh and not the Spirit).

I have been mourning and praying for the Church of America for many years. The church is now in crisis. Foundational truth is not being taught. Various forms of humanism (a philosophical view of man that exalts man over God because of man's intelligence, reason, and cultural achievements) are replacing traditional orthodox Christianity. Man has replaced God as the center of our faith. With the development of the atheistic Western educational system, old theological precepts have been challenged; men no longer rely on the scholarship of the ancient church councils, the reformers, Puritan divines, or more recent biblical scholars. Men now believe they can interpret Scripture anew without any reference to the foundational teaching of our church fathers, creeds, or confessions. With man as the center, we have a type of "pick and choose" Christianity, greatly influenced by the prevailing culture. Right and wrong is largely decided in a biblical intellectual scholarship vacuum. This has resulted in a moralistic, largely pagan, therapeutic type of deism where man seeks to believe what pleases self.

The American church is largely a product of the Enlightenment. Alexis de Tocqueville, a brilliant French aristocrat, came to America in the early nineteenth century (1831). He came to observe the New American Republic, which at time was called "The American Experiment" In Europe. He published a book of his experiences and insights in two volumes; 1835 and 1840 called *Democracy in America*. He was a keen observer and noted that Americans wanted to escape from imposed systems of any kind and to shake off religious authority. He said, "Religion sustains a successful struggle with the spirit of individual independence which is her most dangerous opponent." He later observed that the concept of civil equality "suggests to Americans the idea of the indefinite perfectibility of man," or that man in his imperfect nature was slowly improving and obtaining greater good [Humanism]. The pride of great accomplishments and that independent spirit of America has always been the enemy of the requirement of humility and submission in the Christian faith.

De Tocqueville observed that Americans "wanted to seek by themselves and in themselves for the only reason for things, looking to results without getting entangled in the means toward them." In other words, Americans were very pragmatic and did not need external divine guidance to discover truth. This intense individualism and egotism has resulted in a shift from church tradition, collective beliefs and creeds to an individual religious experience. Americans don't what to be saved by a sovereign God. They want to save themselves. Americans see themselves as spiritual, but not religious. It is just God and me!

The nineteenth century was an era of increasing liberalism. First with the transcendentalism of the Boston liberals such as Emerson who taught the "Highest revelation is that God is in every man." This was followed in Europe with the rise of "higher criticism" of the German scholars, which was a liberal deconstruction of Scripture. Karl Barth, a Swiss theologian, (1886-1968) rebelled against the German theologians and summarized theological liberalism as, "*a God without wrath (bringing) men without sin into a kingdom without judgment through the ministration of a Christ without a cross.*" Unfortunately, very little has changed since these words were penned early in the early twentieth century.

A recent book by Christian Smith and Melinda Denton called *Soul Searching: The Religious and Spiritual Eyes of American Teenagers,* Oxford University Press 2005, explores the very heart of the American teen. The authors took part in a National Study of Youth and Religion and concluded that today's youth can be best characterized as having a *Moralistic Therapeutic Deism* consisting of these five beliefs.

1. "A god exists who created and ordered the world and watches over human life on earth."

2. "God wants people to be good, nice, and fair to each other as taught in the Bible and by most world religions."
3. "The central goal of life is to be happy and to feel good about oneself."
4. "God does not need to be particularly involved in one's life except when God is needed to resolve a problem."
5. "Good people go to heaven when they die."

The average American teenager "believes in God and such" but has only a very superficial understanding of theological concepts such as "what is repentance or saving faith?" They are very individualistic and they believe in "whatever?" The dominant religion among American teens is about feeling good, happy, secure, getting along amiably with people, being at peace, and being able to resolve problems. This is becoming the dominant civil religion in young people who are destined to be the future leaders in America.

The religious experience has now become about "finding self" and is authenticated often by a quasi-religious experience. This book is a twenty-first century re-examination of "The American Experiment."

I would like to give you some telling statistics about the dramatic changes that have occurred in the last fifty years. We now live in a post Christian society where the church is becoming increasingly irrelevant. Various pollsters have estimated that 75 percent of Americans were Christians in 1950 and 35 percent in the 1970s. In today's young generation only 15 percent claim to be Christian. Of those in college who began as "Christians," 80 percent will lose their faith by the time they complete college. According to the Barna Research Group at barna.org: "since the 1950s, however, mainline churches have fallen on hard times, declining from more than 80,000 churches to about 72,000 today. The growth among evangelical and Pentecostal churches since the 1950s, combined with the shrinking of the mainline sector, has diminished mainline churches to just one-fifth of all Protestant congregations today. In the past fifty years, mainline church membership dropped by more than one-quarter to roughly twenty million people. Adult church attendance indicates that only 15 percent of all American adults associate with a mainline church these days." Many American pastors are leaving the ministry. It is estimated that only 10 percent of pastors who have begun pastoring will still be in ministry at age sixty-five.

"The tenuous ties that millions of mainline adults have with their church are exemplified by their willingness to consider other spiritual options. Just half (49 percent) describe themselves as "absolutely committed to Christianity." Slightly more (51 percent) are willing to try a new church. Two-thirds (67 percent) are open to pursuing faith in environments or structures that are different from those of a typical church. Almost three-quarters (72 percent) say they are more likely to develop their own religious beliefs than to adopt those taught by their church. And nine out of ten (86 percent) sense that God is motivating people to stay connected to Him through different means and experiences than in the past. Less than half contend that the Bible is accurate in the life principles it teaches. Only half of all mainline adults say that they are on a personal quest for spiritual truth. And when asked to identify their highest priority in life, less than one out of every ten mainline Protestants placed their faith as their highest priority.

"Faith remains a hot topic in America these days," George Barna commented at barna.org and expanding on the theme. "Politicians, athletes, cultural philosophers, teachers, entertainers, musicians—nearly everyone has something to say about faith, religion, spirituality, morality, and belief these days. But as the fundamental values and assumptions of our nation continue to shift, so do our ideas about faith and spirituality. Many of our basic assumptions are no longer firm or predictable.

"One of those assumptions relates to how we develop our faith. These days," he continued, "the faith arena is a marketplace from which we get ideas, beliefs, relationships, habits, rituals and traditions that make immediate sense to us, and with which we are comfortable. The notion of associating with a particular faith—whether it is Christianity, Judaism, Islam, or some other strain—still has appeal because that connection provides a discernible identity and facilitates the possibility of belonging to something meaningful. But the actual components of what we choose to belong to are driven by our momentary needs and perceptions, i.e. adults (9 percent) say some aspect of faith constitutes their top priority.

"Meanwhile the Charismatic/Pentecostal churches are growing. A decade ago, three out of ten adults claimed to be charismatic or Pentecostal Christians. Today, 36 percent of Americans accept that designation. That corresponds to approximately eighty million adults. (For the Barna survey, this included people who said they were a charismatic or Pentecostal Christian, that they had been 'filled with the Holy Spirit' and who said they believe that 'the charismatic gifts, such as tongues, deliverance, and healing, are still valid and active today.')

"Charismatics are found throughout the fabric of American Christianity. Although just 8 percent of the population is evangelical, half of evangelical adults (49 percent) fit the charismatic definition. A slight majority of all born again Christians (51 percent) is charismatic. Nearly half of all adults who attend a Protestant church (46 percent) are charismatic." For more demographic information on the state of the church please go to George Barna at <u>barna.org</u>

I am a Charismatic Christian of the reformed Baptist theological tradition. I love my charismatic friends and I have been blessed greatly by their fellowship and many of their churches. However, many charismatic churches have strayed from the centrality of the gospel. Their concepts of spirituality are very fuzzy, amorphous, and problematic without reference to biblical propositional truth. The search for spirituality has opened many to anything that seems spiritual, including a host of neo-pagan Gnostic beliefs, including shamanism, astrology, kabbalah, and spiritual techniques derived from pagan, African, East Indian, and Chinese spirituality. They have focused on "experiences of the Holy Spirit" rather than "experience the Trinity of God" the center. Any focus on Jesus only, the gifts of the Holy Spirit only, or focus on the Father, as creator God, only, can lead to heresy and is out of biblical balance.

Oswald Chambers warns us in his beloved book *My Utmost for His Highest* in the chapter for July 20th that: "When we are in an unhealthy state physically or emotionally, we always want thrills. In the physical domain this will lead to counterfeiting the Holy Ghost; in the emotional life it leads to inordinate affection and the destruction of morality; and in the spiritual domain if we insist on getting thrills, on mounting up with wings, it will end in the destruction of spirituality."[1]

Perhaps it is the lack of discernment that troubles me the most about some charismatic churches. The hijacking of many well-meaning people by the "prosperity teaching," focus on the "prophetic," and the "signs and wonders teaching" is particularly tragic and reflects on the very weak theological foundation of many charismatic churches. The focus on experiences with the Holy Spirit is no substitute for solid exegesis (interpretation) of Scripture. There is a balance. It is focused on biblical discipleship in the Word and the Spirit.

Many pagan religions speak in tongues and also have genuine signs and wonders. Naïve, vulnerable Christians think the miraculous must come from God because it is so spiritual. They have not been taught about the reality of demonic deception and can easily be captivated by it. Chinese Brother Watchman Nee used to see many spiritual manifestations in his primarily pagan and Buddhist Chinese culture. When his disciples would come excited by some alleged miracle; he would ask: "What was the source? Was it God, or a demonic miracle?" We need to ask the same question today! We are not to believe every spirit.

> "Beloved, do not believe every spirit, but test the
> spirits to see whether they are from God, for many
> false prophets have gone out into the world. By
> this you know the Spirit of God: every spirit that
> confesses that Jesus Christ has come in the flesh is

---

[1] Oswald Chambers, *My Utmost For His Highest* (Grand Rapids, MI: Discovery House Publishers, 1935 by Dodd Mead, renewed 1963 by the Oswald Chambers Publications Assn., LTD).

from God, and every spirit that does not confess Jesus is not from God. This is the spirit of the antichrist, which you heard was coming and now is in the world already." (1 John 4:1-3)

Finally, I have chosen to use the words man, men, him, himself for mankind rather than say men and women for purposes of simplicity. Many of my comments are purposely short and terse to allow the Holy Spirit to expand the meaning and spiritual illusion for the reader. There is a large amount of unreferenced Scripture used in the main text. I have chosen to let the reader find some of the biblical reference sites for himself. All Bible quotations are from the English Standard Bible (ESV) only.

There is something in this small book to offend nearly everybody! I desire not to offend but to warn God's people of the deception present in the American church. We live in a day where there has been an epidemic of moral failure among Christian leaders. This book is not a witch-hunt. I have chosen certain ministries for characterization because they are examples of the major deception present in the church today. Many Christians have been so disappointed with some Christian leaders and their ministries that they no longer attend traditional churches. Many are now part of the rapidly growing house church movement.

I have used a lot of hyperbole or exaggerated statements and claims not to be taken literally but to be used for teaching purposes. Purposely, I have tried to minimize the use of names of church leaders, denominations, or ministries. The book portrays types and shadows of the American Church by using allegory. I am constantly reminded that my treatment of controversial subjects may hurt my dearest brothers in the Lord whose piety and walk with the Lord I have the deepest respect.

I am a physician and I know that there can be no cure without an accurate diagnosis. The American church is very sick and an accurate assessment of her illness is needed. This requires undressing the patient and exposing sensitive and embarrassing areas. The physician prods and probes and the patient complains and says, "Ouch, you are hurting me doctor!" A thorough evaluation can be painful. Only then can the proper diagnosis be made to determine if a cure is possible.

Those who desire to follow our Lord will repent and receive correction if the Holy Spirit speaks to their heart. Others may agree or disagree with the contents of this book. I can only humbly share what I see and hear and see very imperfectly. Jesus offended all the religious rulers of His day, as did the Old Testament prophets. Finally, many are concerned with the declining spiritual condition of American society. The Christian leadership largely blames the encroachment of humanism and liberalism, as taught in the American educational and political establishment, for the increasing moral failure in America. The problem lies largely at the feet of the American church and Christian leaders need largely to take responsibility, cry out to God, and repent. Christians are called to be salt and light and we have failed miserably. This book examines various heresies to demonstrate the vulnerable condition of the church due to lack of discernment and shallow understanding of the deeper truths of God. The book presents problems and solutions.

It seems so ironic when pagan secular men grasp the larger picture of the greatness of God then Christians! My prayer is that those who read this book will tremble and fear before our Lord and worship Him, the Living God who endures forever, and grow in appreciation of His greatness.

Then King Darius wrote to all the peoples, nations, and languages that dwell in all the earth: "Peace be multiplied to you. I make a decree, that in all my royal dominion people are to tremble and fear before the God of Daniel, for **he is the living God, enduring forever; his kingdom shall never be destroyed, and his dominion shall be to the end. He delivers and rescues; he works signs and wonders in heaven and on earth, he who has saved Daniel from the power of the lions.**" *(Daniel 6:25-27)*

Chapter 1

GOSPEL COMPROMISE

I have been a Christian for nearly forty years and have had a wealth of church experiences. I love God's children and His Church. I have witnessed the gradual deterioration of the most basic understanding of the Gospel of Christ. Churches are tossed too and fro in the sea of humanity, traveling in circles while moving further away from the Promised Land and Heaven beyond. This book is about my story, dreams, and visions written largely in allegorical form. It is a warning to those caught in heretical churches and doctrines to leave and repent. My dreams or visions are in bold type in order to separate the vision from the accompanying comments.

I awoke, as if in a dream, but my surroundings were so real, I knew that this was no ordinary dream. I was in the ocean at night. I was cold and wet and holding on to just a piece of driftwood as I was tossed around by waves. Then I saw a huge ship ahead and as it came closer I yelled out, "Help me!" Someone saw me and threw me a line and pulled me on board. The ship was huge, a mega ship called *"Easy Grace."* Its homeport was Laodicea, Turkey. My guide told me that this ship was "seeker sensitive" and had something for everybody. They had basketball courts and tennis courts and swimming pools and a rock climbing location. They had Starbucks coffee shops scattered throughout the ship and the coffee was free!

1

Some of the passengers were seasick and I tried to help but was told to let the crew take care of it. After all that is what they were paid for. Evidently the cruise was very expensive but the money was being used for a good cause. The collection was taken each night to help those less fortunate so that they could join others on a similar sister ship for another cruise.

I was told that this was a Christian ship and the pastor had a message that did not offend, but made everybody feel better. It was a message that was man-centered and not God-centered. As I walked through the ship I went outside and saw two men that evidently were being extremely sexually intimate. I asked my guide about the appropriateness of this and he told me not to worry and to stop being judgmental. He explained to me that people on the ship came from a variety of social and religious backgrounds and they were just transitioning to the Christian life. Their goal was to keep people happy, build self-esteem, and avoid controversial issues. I was very offended by this answer and asked him if there wasn't an absolute standard of behavior for Christians? He explained that the church leadership never uses the word "absolute," since it suggests a rigid mindset and doesn't take into consideration peoples' individual psychosocial problems. I then responded if there is no absolute truth there could be no Christianity!

The church staffer angrily exclaimed that the Bible forbids judging anyone in Matthew 7:1. *"Judge (Greek krino) not, that you be not judged. For with the judgment you pronounce you will be judged, and with the measure you use it will be measured to you."*

I responded that the Greek word *krino* is best translated from the context to mean not to condemn, censure or pass judgment on, as well as discern guilt or innocence. We are not to judge the world but are called to judge the church! We are called by Paul in 1 Corinthians to discern the world around us and pray for repentance for the lost.

"For though absent in body, I am present in spirit; and as if present, I have already pronounced judgment (krino) on the one who did such a thing. When you are assembled in the name of the Lord Jesus

and my spirit is present, with the power of our Lord Jesus, you are to deliver this man to Satan for the destruction of the flesh, so that his spirit may be saved in the day of the Lord." (1 Cor. 5:3-5)

Notice Paul uses the same Greek word (*krino*) for judgment. Does this mean that Paul was disobeying Christ's command in Matthew 7:1 not to judge? Of course not! Jesus said in John 7:24, *"Do not judge by appearances, but judge with right judgment."*

We are to discern evil and pass judgment in the church but are not called to judge the secular world. God will judge those outside of His Church. Paul tells the Corinthian Church that they must judge those inside of the church.

"When one of you has a grievance against another, does he dare go to law before the unrighteous instead of the saints? Or do you not know that the saints will judge (krino) the world? And if the world is to be judged by you, are you incompetent to try trivial cases? Do you not know that we are to judge (krino) angels? How much more, then, matters pertaining to this life!" (1 Cor. 6:1-3)

There was sin in the Corinthian church and the church body tolerated it rather than dealing with it and excommunicating the guilty fornicator. Does this sound familiar?

I explained that Christians are called to discern evil and to judge it in the Church, to the limited extent given in the Word of God, realizing that God is the ultimate judge of all things and He will pass the ultimate judgment on every sin.

> *"Partiality in judging is not good. Whoever says to the wicked, "You are in the right," will be cursed by peoples, abhorred by nations, but those who rebuke the wicked will have delight, and a good blessing will come upon them."* (Prov. 24:23-25)

"How many Christians have been injured by the failure of church leaders to discipline sinners in the church?" I asked. It seems so ironic that there is more mercy shown to the perpetrator of evil than the victims in many churches. This should not be so!

One man's sin, the sin of Achan brought defeat to the whole nation of Israel in Joshua 7:10-26. God's response was to call out the people to find the perpetrator and kill him.

"Israel has sinned; they have transgressed my covenant that I commanded them; they have taken some of the devoted things; they have stolen and lied and put them among their own belongings. Therefore the people of Israel cannot stand before their enemies. They turn their backs before their enemies, because they have become devoted for destruction. I will be with you no more, unless you destroy the devoted things from among you. Get up! Consecrate the people and say, 'Consecrate yourselves for tomorrow; for thus says the Lord, God of Israel, "There are devoted things in your midst, O Israel. <u>You cannot stand before your enemies until you take away the devoted things from among you</u>." (Josh. 7:11-12)

"Take no part in the unfruitful works of darkness, but instead expose them." (Eph. 5:11)

"Do not be unequally yoked with unbelievers. For what partnership has righteousness with lawlessness? Or what fellowship has light with darkness? What accord has Christ with Belial? Or what portion does a believer share with an unbeliever? What agreement has the temple of God with idols? For we are the temple of the living God." (2 Cor. 6:14-16)

I wondered how much of the weakness of the church today is due to its failure to discern and remove idolatry and idol worshipers from the church or how many great ships at sea have been sunk by the failure to deal appropriately with one man's sin. I remembered the words of Peter:

> "For it is time for judgment to begin at the household of God; and if it begins with us, what will be the outcome for those who do not obey the gospel of God? And "If the righteous is scarcely saved, what will become of the ungodly and the sinner?" (1 Pet. 4:17-18)

Paul also shared in love about his passion for church discipline.

> *"But if we judged ourselves truly, we would not be judged. But when we are judged by the Lord, we are disciplined so that we may not be condemned along with the world."* (1 Cor. 11:31-32)

My guide became quite angry and told me that I was a bigot and proceeded to grab me by the collar to throw me overboard! I considered myself to have been very fortunate since soon after I was thrown overboard the ship Easy Grace seemed to hit a rock and began to sink. There was much confusion since this ship was thought to be unsinkable. The band played continuous gospel music as the ship was sinking. The people on board relied on the paid staff to get them into lifeboats and to save them, but the staff was very frightened and they took the best lifeboats for themselves and deserted the passengers.

I hadn't been in the water very long before an old rusty sailboat came by called the 3T. In small letters it said *Trouble, Tribulation, and Trials*. Its homeport was Biblos, Greece. The ship looked quite old, as if it had made many passages in the sea. The crew of the 3T threw me a life preserver that I grasped tightly. I felt the strong current pulling on my clothing so eventually as I was pulled towards the sailing ship I arrived naked with no possessions. The ship itself was filled with joy in spite of evidence of some obvious deprivation. The crew gladly stripped off some of their clothing to give to me. You could sense peace and love immediately when I arrived on the ship. A great storm had arisen but there was no fear on the ship and they trusted their Captain to bring them through the storm.

As the "3Ts" sailed on, it passed close to the sinking Mega Ship, Easy Grace and I heard the passengers complaining about the desertion of the crew. The passengers had great expectations of a pleasurable cruise and a ticket to heaven. After all, they paid good money for the cruise and expected results!

5

Earlier, while on board the ship, I had spoken to their spiritual leaders and the Captain of the ship and the crew had preached a message of a way to heaven without pain or suffering. The ship's Captain admitted that while repentance was necessary it would come later and just gradually. To them, repentance meant only a changed mind and not changed behavior. Their message was "just believe." "Believe what?" I had asked. Everyone on the Easy Grace glared at me for asking such a stupid question. They said, "Of course, it's to believe in Jesus." I responded, "If you believe in Jesus you will be saved!" I quipped, "But doesn't it also say in the book of James (2:19) that the 'demons believe and tremble?' **The demons believe so won't they be saved too?" I questioned. They glared at me and had no answer.**

They were told that if you believe that Jesus is the Son of God, and that Jesus came to earth to save man, and died on the cross you could be sure to go to heaven. I asked, "What are we saved from?" They responded with, "Hell of course!" I thought that was certainly true, but what I needed was to be saved from not only the wrath of God, but my self-centeredness and myself. My problem was about having self on the throne of my life rather than God; and all the besetting sins of the self-life such as selfishness, self-centeredness, greed, lust, anger, bitterness, pride, gluttony, sloth, idolatry, jealousy, and impure thoughts. The difference between a head-trip and a heart-trip is so subtle. I thought, so many have confidence in what they believe in their heads rather than the eternal confidence of knowing Jesus in their heart! True faith is relational based on knowing Jesus as a person rather than a faith in the impersonal historical Jesus. True faith involves death to the self-life and a life lived for Christ.

"Then Jesus told his disciples, "If anyone would come after me, let him deny himself and take up his cross and follow me. For whoever would save his life will lose it, but whoever loses his life for my sake will find it." (Matt. 16:24-25)

Chapter 2

CHEAP GRACE

The leaders of **Easy Grace** believed in the substitutionary work of Jesus on the cross for man's salvation and believed that faith without works purchases salvation for the believer. They subtly departed from traditional orthodoxy by teaching that faith alone, in the redemptive work of Christ, was sufficient to purchase a ticket to Heaven! Orthodox teaching has always been that while faith alone, without any of man's works, is all that is needed for salvation, but works, pleasing to God, will always follow a true conversion.

"What good is it, my brothers, if someone says he has faith but does not have works? Can that faith save him? If a brother or sister is poorly clothed and lacking in daily food, and one of you says to them, "Go in peace, be warmed and filled," without giving them the things needed for the body, what good is that? So also faith by itself, if it does not have works, is dead. But someone will say, "You have faith and I have works." Show me your faith apart from your works, and I will show you my faith by my works. You believe that God is one; you do well. Even the demons believe—and shudder! Do you want to be shown, you foolish person, that faith apart from works is useless?" (James 2:14-20)

James does not set faith against works but teaches that saving faith always leads to an obedient lifestyle. The foolish Galatians

7

believed that observance of circumcision and obedience to the Jewish ceremonial law brought righteousness. Paul corrected them in Galatians 5:6: *"For in Christ Jesus neither circumcision nor uncircumcision counts for anything, but only faith working through love."*

Both Paul and James were in agreement that it is by grace alone, which includes repentance and regeneration, followed by saving faith, and without any of man's works that brings salvation; and that true faith working through love always produces works of righteousness. Genuine conversion always bears spiritual fruit. These false leaders taught that there were two types of Christians, carnal or fleshly Christians and spiritual Christians. Some people continue with ongoing sin issues after a "Christian salvation conversion." They thought they were Christians because of their intellectual acceptance of the atoning work of Christ on the cross for their souls, but there had never been true repentance. They had a **Head Trip** or you are what you believe, versus a **Heart Trip**, which is a changed heart that produces changed behavior! Paul responds in Romans 8:5-11:

> *"For those who live according to the flesh set their minds on the things of the flesh, but those who live according to the Spirit set their minds on the things of the Spirit. For to set the mind on the flesh is death, but to set the mind on the Spirit is life and peace. For the mind that is set on the flesh is hostile to God, for it does not submit to God's law; indeed, it cannot. Those who are in the flesh cannot please God. You, however, are not in the flesh but in the Spirit, if in fact the Spirit of God dwells in you. Anyone who does not have the Spirit of Christ does not belong to him. But if Christ is in you, although the body is dead because of sin, the Spirit is life because*

*of righteousness. If the Spirit of him who raised
Jesus from the dead dwells in you, he who raised
Christ Jesus from the dead will also give life to
your mortal bodies through his Spirit who dwells
in you."*

The Bible is very clear; those who are called by His Name,
yet are carnal or live for the flesh are not His! Only those who
have the Spirit of Christ and are led into a life of righteousness
will be saved! This false teaching about the assurance of salvation
of carnal Christians has deceived many. This has produced a false
assurance of salvation for many. How tragic!

The call to follow Jesus is to leave the things of this world
and be separate as He is separate! Man wants to be justified by
good works alone without personal holiness. God's sovereign grace
equips us for a life of holy living for Him.

*"Now this I say and testify in the Lord, that you must no longer
walk as the Gentiles do, in the futility of their minds. They are dark-
ened in their understanding, alienated from the life of God because
of the ignorance that is in them, due to their hardness of heart. They
have become callous and have given themselves up to sensuality,
greedy to practice every kind of impurity. But that is not the way you
learned Christ!— assuming that you have heard about him and were
taught in him, as the truth is in Jesus, to put off your old self, which
belongs to your former manner of life and is corrupt through deceitful desires, and to be renewed in the spirit of your minds, and to put
on the new self, created after the likeness of God in true righteousness
and holiness."* (Eph. 4:17-24)

John Calvin writes that: *"He whose life differs not from that
of unbelievers, has learned nothing of Christ; for the knowledge of
Christ cannot be separated from the mortification of the flesh."*[2]
Wow! A statement rarely heard today.

Holiness is an unpopular word in today's sensual hedonistic
culture but the God of today is the same God of yesterday and
tomorrow. (Heb. 13:8) Luke further reminds us: *that we, being deliv-*

---

[2] (Calvin's Commentaries Ephesians, Baker Books 2009)

ered from the hand of our enemies, might serve him without fear, in holiness and righteousness before him all our days. (Luke 1:74-75)

The message on the mega ship tried to be culturally relevant and avoided any discussion about personal holiness. I thought, what a trap! Any attempt to make the gospel culturally relevant is bound to compromise the message of the gospel. We seem to forget that Jesus wasn't culturally relevant! Cultural accommodation is unnecessary and has never worked throughout history. Jesus was hated because He was not only anti-establishment, but also His message turned the cultural mores of His time upside down. The compromise made by these church leaders was to emphasize certain moral truths while avoiding the deep central truths of the Bible. It was the merchandizing of the Holy! The focus by many of the leaders was building self-esteem in people. I remembered the story in Luke 18:10-14 of the tax collector and the Pharisee.

> "Two men went up into the temple to pray, one a Pharisee and the other a tax collector. The Pharisee, standing by himself, prayed thus: 'God, I thank you that I am not like other men, extortioners, unjust, adulterers, or even like this tax collector. I fast twice a week; I give tithes of all that I get. But the tax collector, standing far off, would not even lift up his eyes to heaven, but beat his breast, saying, 'God, be merciful to me, a sinner!' I tell you, this man went down to his house justified, rather than the other. For everyone who exalts himself will be humbled, but the one who humbles himself will be exalted." (Luke 18:12)

The tax collector exemplified self-loathing and the Pharisee self-centered conceit and lots of self-esteem. The man that was justified was the man with humility and self-loathing, who saw himself as a sinner! Those few examples in Scripture of a man coming into the presence of a Holy God have always produced a Holy awe and humility as in Isaiah 6:4.

"And I said: "Woe is me! For I am lost; for I am a man of unclean lips, and I dwell in the midst of a people of unclean lips; for my eyes have seen the King, the Lord of hosts!"

The message of the cross will never be popular or politically correct. To be culturally relevant as a Christian ministry is so often to be culturally irrelevant to God! Tozer once said:

"Let us plant ourselves on the hill of Zion and invite the world to come over to us, but never under any circumstances will we go over to them. The cross is the symbol of Christianity, and the cross speaks of death and separation, never of compromise. No one ever compromised with a cross. The cross separated between the dead and the living. The timid and the fearful will cry "Extreme!" and they will be right. The cross is the essence of all that is extreme and final. The message of Christ is a call across a gulf from death to life, from sin to righteousness and from Satan to God."3

The message of the certainty of Hell and eternal destruction was avoided since it upset people. The message of eternal damnation was obscured by illusions to universalism (everyone will eventually be saved) and Annihilationism, which is the minority Christian doctrine that sinners are destroyed or annihilated rather than tormented forever in "hell" or the lake of fire. This ancient heretical confusion has been in the church since Origen (185-254) taught that eventually God would restore everything to Himself including Satan. It is directly related to the doctrine of conditional immortality, the idea that a human soul is not immortal unless it is given eternal life. Annihilationism asserts that God will eventually destroy or annihilate the wicked, leaving only the righteous to live on in immortality. Some annihilationists believe the wicked will be punished for their sins in the lake of fire before being annihilated. Others believe that hell is a false doctrine of pagan origin. Annihilationist denominations include the Seventh-day Adventists, Bible Students, Jehovah's Witnesses, Christadelphians and the various Advent Christian churches. Some Protestant and Anglican writers have also proposed annihilationist doctrines. Annihilationists

---

3   (The Set of the Sail, pp 35-36). From the book, *Tozer on Christian Leadership*, published by WingSpread Publishers.

base the doctrine on their exegesis of Scripture, some early church writing, historical criticism of the doctrine of hell, and the concept of God as too loving to punish his creations forever. Annihilationists are quick to point out that spiritual death happens the moment one sins and that it is illogical to believe further separation from God can take place. In addition, annihilationists claim that complete separation from God conflicts the doctrine of omnipresence in which God is present everywhere, including hell. Some annihilationists accept the position that hell is a separation from God by taking the position that God sustains the life of his creations: when separated from God, one simply ceases to exist. Opponents of annihilationism often argue that ceasing to exist is not eternal punishment and therefore conflicts with passages such as Matthew 25:46: *"And these shall go away into everlasting punishment but the righteous into eternal life."*

"And they shall go out and look on the dead bodies of the men who have rebelled against me. For the worm shall not die, their fire shall not be quenched." (Isa. 66:24)

There is the concept of what is called "ultimate reconciliation" among theologians. It means that ultimately the punishment of the wicked will be worked out in some fashion or another so that everyone will be reconciled with God and go to heaven. Some believe that because of the sacrifice of Jesus on the cross, followed by His resurrection, that this purchased ultimate reconciliation from God for all men. We will be one big human family! Of course, these speculations have absolutely no biblical foundation. The redemptive work of Christ was a "peculiar redemption" where He justified and redeemed only those chosen before the foundation of the world to be His. Only a few will be saved. Many will be lost. The last shall be first!

"And Jesus looked around and said to his disciples, "How difficult it will be for those who have wealth to enter the kingdom of God!" And the disciples were amazed at his words. But Jesus said to them again, "Children, how difficult it is to enter the kingdom of God! It is easier for a camel to go through the eye of a needle than for a rich person to enter the kingdom of God." And they were exceedingly

astonished, and said to him, "Then who can be saved?" Jesus looked at them and said, "With man it is impossible, but not with God. For all things are possible with God." Peter began to say to him, "See, we have left everything and followed you." Jesus said, "Truly, I say to you, there is no one who has left house or brothers or sisters or mother or father or children or lands, for my sake and for the gospel, who will not receive a hundredfold now in this time, houses and brothers and sisters and mothers and children and lands, with persecutions, and in the age to come eternal life. But many who are first will be last, and the last first." (Mark 10:23-31)

We live in a Post-Christian world where we believe what we want to believe and avoid the hard truths of Scripture. A recent book by David Campbell of Notre Dame and Robert Putman of Harvard reported, "Nearly two-thirds of evangelicals under thirty-five believe non-Christians can go to heaven, vs. 39 percent of those over sixty-five." (<u>American Grace: How Religion Divides Us.</u> Simon and Schuster 2010) Jesus said that: *"I am the way, and the truth, and the life. <u>No one comes to the Father except through me</u>!"* (John 14:6) The fact that Jesus is the only way to salvation seems to the post-modern man much too exclusive, racist, and intolerant of those "good, godly people of other religions!"

"Enter by the narrow gate. For the gate is wide and the way is easy that leads to destruction, and <u>those who enter by it are many</u>. For the gate is narrow and the way is hard that leads to life, and <u>those who find it are few</u>." (Matt. 7:13-14)

The good news is that by the grace and providence of God some will be saved. The bad news is most will be lost; non-regenerative man faces eternal damnation and torment in the flames of Hell. A leader who presents only the good news is presenting only half the gospel. What makes man think he can present only part of the gospel? Church leaders are often more afraid of offending man then offending God. After all, isn't He a loving and forgiving God? He couldn't possibly send good people to hell; could He? Yes, hell is full of nice, good, upstanding citizens! He is a God of wrath and judgment who will hold all men responsible, particularly church leaders, for not preaching the whole council of God.

A crewman of the 3Ts said to me that "Heaven is full of sinners and hell is full of good people!" I pondered that statement for some time before I understood what he had said. Jesus said:

> *"Go and learn what this means, 'I desire mercy, and not sacrifice.' For I came not to call the righteous, but sinners."* (Matt. 9:13)

Jesus did not come to save the righteous but sinners. Only sinners will go to heaven. If we cannot see our sin then we don't need a savior! If we don't see our sin then there can be no repentance. If there is no work of repentance and change then there has been no salvation!

> *"Just so, I tell you, there will be more joy in heaven over one sinner who repents than over ninety-nine righteous persons who need no repentance."* (Luke 15:7)

> *"But God shows his love for us in that while we were still sinners, Christ died for us."* (Rom. 5:8)

If heaven is full of sinners then hell must be full of good people or the self-righteous. Jesus spoke to the self-righteous religious rulers in Israel. *"You serpents, you brood of vipers, how are you to escape being sentenced to hell?"* (Matt. 23:33) Yes, hell is full of the religious and the self-righteous who think that because they are good people, believe in God, and do good works, that this earns them the right to go to heaven!

The Holy Spirit had convicted me of my sin and I had repented of my self-centered life and had called on God's mercy and grace and had received saving faith many years ago. I knew that deep in my heart my relationship with God was requiring so much more from me. True faith costs and demands everything!

> *"And calling the crowd to him with his disciples, he
> said to them, "If anyone would come after me, let
> him deny himself and take up his cross and follow
> me. For whoever would save his life will lose it,
> but whoever loses his life for my sake and the
> gospel's will save it. For what does it profit a man
> to gain the whole world and forfeit his soul? For
> what can a man give in return for his soul? For
> whoever is ashamed of me and of my words in
> this adulterous and sinful generation, of him will
> the Son of Man also be ashamed when he comes
> in the glory of his Father with the holy angels."*
> (Mark 8:34-38)

I knew that true faith is radical faith, and costs everything. It requires a radical change in the believer. Radical faith without radical change in the believer is false faith. I experienced that true faith and it changed me. My relationships with my family, friends, fellow workers, and the world around me also changed. I experienced that many of my friends and some of my family had deserted me and called me a fool, crazy, and a religious freak. When I told my fellow workers that I had become a Christian they mocked me, laughed at me, and eventually drove me out of the workplace.

The cost of my salvation was the very death of God's only son. If it cost God everything that He treasured, then I knew that it would cost me everything also. It was costly grace and not cheap grace that was calling to me. I knew that I had been transformed by Christ (2 Cor. 5:17) yet this was just the beginning of a lifetime of many trials. I was beginning to understand that while conversion was a one-time event after I became born again, it was just the beginning of the process of my personal sanctification, which would be accompanied by many trials, troubles, and tribulations. I thought of so many who claimed to be converted yet rejected the discipline of God and the pain of transformation!

"Therefore, if anyone is in Christ, he is a new creation. The old has passed away; behold, the new has come. All this is from God, who through Christ reconciled us to himself and gave us the ministry of reconciliation; that is, in Christ God was reconciling the world to himself, not counting their trespasses against them, and entrusting to us the message of reconciliation. Therefore, we are ambassadors for Christ, God making his appeal through us. We implore you on behalf of Christ, be reconciled to God. For our sake he made him to be sin who knew no sin, so that in him we might become the righteousness of God." (2 Cor. 5:17-21)

I looked back at the mega ship *Easy Grace* and saw many people floating in the sea with life preservers that were stenciled with a message, "Cheap Grace." My heart was broken and I mourned for those caught up in the waves since I knew that when storms came they would drown. They had invested in a very strong steel ship that was a magnificent structure and thought to be unsinkable. It had the latest and best technology. They were sure that their ship would never sink and would endure the worst of storms. After all, their ship was the largest, wealthiest, and most respected ship in their city. Their pastor was on the radio and even had his own television show.

They were sure that God was blessing them since he had obviously allowed them to build this great ship. They were socially conscious and concerned about global warming, AIDS, hunger, immigration, and against torture. Their gospel was consumer driven and user friendly. Religion was a commodity about self-fulfillment or about finding self rather than losing self. Some called their ship **The Great Hope**, others said it should be called **The Great Hoax**. I did not see or hear of the cross on the ship. I knew that without the cross, theirs was **False Hope**.

The name "Easy Grace" reminded me of the words of the great German Lutheran Christian martyr killed by Hitler in 1945 by the name of Dietrich Bonhoeffer, whose book *The Cost of Discipleship* was written in German in 1937. It was very prophetic since Bonhoeffer's faith would cost him everything, including his life. *"Cheap grace means grace sold on the market like cheapjacks wares. The sacraments, the forgiveness of sin, and the consolations of religion are thrown away at cut prices. Grace is represented as God's inexhaustible treasury, from which he showers blessings with generous hands, without asking questions or fixing limits. Grace without price; grace without cost! The essence of grace, we suppose, is that the account has been paid in advance; and because it has been paid everything can be had for nothing. Since the cost was infinite, the possibilities of using and spending it are infinite. What would grace be if it were not Cheap?...***Cheap grace therefore amounts to a denial of the living word of God, in fact, a denial of the incarnation of the word of God. Cheap grace means the justification of sin without justification of the sinner."...***"Cheap grace is preaching forgiveness without requiring repentance, baptism without church discipline, communion without confession, absolution without personal confession. Cheap grace is grace without discipleship, grace without the cross, grace without Jesus Christ, living and incarnate.*** Costly grace is the treasure hidden in the field; for the sake of it man will gladly go and sell all that he has. It is the pearl of great price to buy which the merchant will sell all of his goods. It is the Kingly rule of Christ, for whose sake man will pluck out the eye which causes him to stumble, it is the call of Jesus Christ at which the disciple leaves his nets and follows Him... Costly grace is the gospel which must be sought again and again, the gift which must be asked for, the door at which a man must knock."*[4]

"If anyone would come after me, let him deny himself and take up his cross and follow me. For whoever would save his life will lose it, but whoever loses his life for my sake will find it. For what will it profit a man if he gains the whole world and forfeits his soul?" (Matt. 16:24-25)

---

[4] Dietrich Bonhoeffer, *The Cost of Discipleship* (New York: Touchstone Books, 1995), 43-45.

Grace is not cheap since it cost God the life of His only son on the cross. Grace is not easy either since it requires man to give up all and follow Him. Costly grace is the grace of Christian discipline, discipleship, and personal obedience, which calls us to lay our lives down for Christ. It is costly because it cost God the sacrifice of His son and will cost us our lives also. The call to deny self and lay down oneself at the cross is rarely heard in the church today; instead the call is to find yourself, instead of losing oneself in Christ. I looked at the sinking ship and cried out to God for mercy on so many deceived people.

Others had made it into lifeboats as the band played on. I could hear some shouting about the promise of being raptured in times of difficulty. Their pastor had promised freedom from suffering and pain. He promised peace, safety, prosperity, and security. They were to trust in him because he had talked with Jesus and he promised that he would take them through any storms ahead. They seemed confident that when great storms would come they would be protected or raptured away from any difficulty and suffering. Just then I saw a huge wave come and swamp their lifeboats and it appeared that all had drowned.

Some of the passengers in other lifeboats mocked our poor little sailing ship. Our ship seemed to be a collective failure about to happen. It was rusty and damaged and appeared to be destined for the scrap yard. The comment was made that unsightly ships, like ours, should be scrapped since they were a disgrace to the general maritime community. They didn't seem to recognize that our ship was a Christian ship because they couldn't understand the message on our stern of tribulation, trials, and troubles.

Our ship was much stronger than it appeared from its external condition. The ship was amazingly flexible in that it bent with the waves so it could not be broken by the heaviest seas. Other ships were very rigid which made them easily broken in half when they faced great waves.

I saw many dead people floating in the sea enclosed in life rings that spoke of their theology. They were labeled gnosticism, armenianism, dispensationalism, pre-millennial-pretrib-

ulation rapturism, postmodernism, sacrementalism, existential-ism, rationalism, humanism, pragmatism, deism, and a variety of other isms. I saw that theology alone, while very import-ant, could not save man. Others were clinging to life rings that said "The Bible, the Word of God." My heart was broken as it observed that many had held tightly to their Bibles and thought their Bible would save them. I knew in my heart that it's the Author of the Bible, God Himself who saves us! I understood personally how easy it was to be convinced that knowledge of the Bible was equal to knowledge of the Lord of the Bible. I thought about the professors and theologians in the many Bible schools who knew the Bible backwards and forwards and thought they could justify themselves by their knowledge of the things of God. I certainly could relate to these theologians because of my own arrogance and pride.

My own knowledge of the Bible had become an idol. I incor-rectly thought if I new the Bible that I understood God. I was reminded of the simplicity of the Bible. Augustine (354-430 AD), Bishop of Hippo, issued the maxim in Latin *"Credo ut intelligam"* which is translated as; *I believe in order to understand.* Once we have saving faith, the Holy Spirit opens our understanding of Scripture. The Holy Spirit must renew the mind before the Word of God becomes understandable. The Bible is about the author of the Bible, God Himself. It is not merely a historical book about God and His people, but is the voice of God or what the ancients called the *Vox Dei* (voice of God). The Bible is the Great Chart Book to guide us through the sea of life and to introduce us to the Author, who wants to tell us about Himself and to speak to us through His Word.

It is only when we have bowed the knee, repented of our sins, and come to a saving relationship with our Lord, Jesus Christ; that God can speak to us through his Word. As I reflected on the Word of God I began to understand that the Bible is like a mirror. As I looked in the mirror I could observe my own sin and hopelessness, reflect on my bad choices, my arrogance, and my idolatry. It was in that mirror of Scripture, I saw there was no hope in self-reformation, but instead, my hope had to be in the mercy and grace of our Lord Jesus. I saw that I could not save myself and that my good works were like wood, hay, and straw that would eventually be judged by the fire of God. I had come to understand that the Bible was not an end to itself but a means to come to know the Author, God Himself, where I was to bow the knee, listen, and learn obedience. I was reminded about my own arrogance in attempts to use the Bible and its precepts, in order to manipulate God! I had to repent and focus on what God was saying to me through His Word as well as what He was saying about Himself.

When we know the Lord and His Word we begin to develop a "Christian Worldview."

Jesus tells us *He is the truth* (John 14:6). Without certain truth there can be no discernment and without discernment there is confusion and vulnerability to deception. The Bible is God's Word to mankind and contains that which is *"profitable for teaching, for reproof, for correction, and for training in righteousness, that the man of God may be competent, equipped for every good work"* (2 Tim. 3:16-17). The test for truth is that a teaching, word, life lived, or prophecy is consistent with Scripture. If we do not know and study God's word we are open to deception!

The more we immerse ourselves in the word of God, the more God's truth will fill us.

"Finally, brothers, whatever is true, whatever is honorable, whatever is just, whatever is pure, whatever is lovely, whatever is commendable, if there is any excellence, if there is anything worthy of praise, think about these things." (Phil. 4:8) The more we immerse ourselves in God's word the more we will know truth. The more truth we know the more we will discern error! Unfortunately, the increasing deception of the church reflects simply on its failure to study truth as revealed in the Bible.

Many who claim to be filled with the Holy Spirit lack significant spiritual discernment; how can this be? One of God's purposes of being filled with the Holy Spirit is to have the Spirit of Truth bring discernment. *"Look carefully then how you walk, not as unwise but as wise, making the best use of the time, because the days are* evil. *Therefore do not be foolish, but understand what the will of the Lord is. And do not get drunk with wine, for that is debauchery, but be filled with the Spirit."* (Eph. 5:15-18) Getting drunk in the spirit is no substitute for being immersed in God's word. When we saturate our minds with Scripture our knowledge of truth deepens. We desire to know God more and serve Him.

Bernard Clairvaux (1090-1153) said, "Some seek knowledge for the sake of knowledge. That is curiosity. Some seek knowledge to be known by others. That is vanity. Some seek knowledge to serve. That is love." If we love God and desire to serve Him we will cherish and be guided by His Word.

Chapter 3

TRUE AND FALSE REPENTANCE

My heart was broken when I reflected on my own attempts of self-reformation and good works. I couldn't understand that I couldn't save myself; only God could save me! The miracle of regeneration is something that God did sovereignly for which I could take no credit. I knew that once I met our Lord in heaven that I could not boast in anything of myself, including my choice to serve Him. He saved me, He did it all, and to Him I would give all the glory. I could only boast in His grace alone! I began to understand that the Bible calls man to troubles and trials designed to purify him. Suffering expands our relationship with God whose purpose is to make God Himself our center and thereby glorify Him. We are called to die daily, but in so doing we become more like our savior. I saw that my salvation produces a never-ending process of growth and trials that slowly unfolds over a lifetime. When we fall, we are picked up by our Savior and encouraged to press on until we finish the race set before us. Our hope is in the hand that holds our hand when we stumble in this life. If we could let go of His hand, we would surely perish, yet we know He will never let go of us.

In the contemporary church salvation has become a very individual, intellectual assent of the historical Jesus. It is a free gift that costs nothing yet promises fire insurance! The true experience with the Lord Jesus, the Father, and Holy Spirit requires obedience, submission, repentance, and true humility. It requires Bible study and understanding propositional truth. It requires death to the old man and things of this world to become conformed to the image of Christ.

While pondering these things, I saw another man floating in the sea grasping a life ring like the ones that saved me. He cried out loudly calling for help. He had difficulty holding onto the life ring tightly and to my dismay he eventually let go and was last seen being enveloped by a large wave. I asked our crewman what happened and he said that the man did not have godly sorrow for his sins and never sought true repentance. He explained to me that true repentance precedes a changed heart. The life ring only saves those who have seen the tragedy of their own life and have called to God for repentance, faith, and forgiveness. It is only then that they can receive true salvation and the fellowship of God. I pondered his words and asked him, "What is true repentance?" He responded that it is not just turning from our sins, but turning away from our old self, life, and dying to our old ways, death to self, friends, family, and position, the acceptance of and adulation of men, wealth, or anything that would distract us from wholehearted passion for God. This includes innocent things like sports, travel, vacations, pursuit of happiness, or anything else that distracts us and takes time away from the Lord.

Repentance is best summarized by what he called the *5 Rs*. They are *Remorse, Renunciation, Reversal, Restitution, and Reliance on God*. False repentance sees behavior as the problem rather than the sin nature. There may be a changed mind because of fear of consequences. This may lead to self-reformation, which may produce self-righteousness. There is a reliance on strength of self or the power within man rather than God's power. A heart convicted by sin doesn't hate sin but a heart broken for sin hates sin. The proof of true repentance is a changed life rather than only changed actions. Repentance is not a one-time experience but a lifetime experience of turning from our sin and selfishness toward our Lord. As we grow in God, His holiness shines like a bright light. The light exposes our true condition before a Holy God. This produces humility and continuous repentance. Paul called himself the least of the Apostles and the greatest sinner of all. David cries out to God in repentance after Nathan, the prophet confronts him about his adultery with Bathsheba in Psalm 51. David saw that self-reformation was impossible. He needed God to *"blot out his transgressions and wash him thoroughly from his iniquity and cleanse him from his sin"* (Ps. 51:1, 2). Not only did God have to purge him from his sin but *"create in him a clean heart and renew His steadfast spirit with in him"* (Ps. 51:10). David understood that true repentance is supernatural. It requires a broken heart and spirit that admits personal sin and has genuine *remorse* for sin. This is followed by *renunciation,* not only of a specific sin, but acknowledging our hopeless sin nature. *Reversal* or a 180 degree turn around, *restitution* where possible, and then *reliance* on God are essential components of biblical repentance. We must believe like David that God will not despise a broken and contrite heart but show mercy to the sinner.

Another crewman told me the story of Zacchaeus the tax collector, in Luke 19:8-9, and his confession to Jesus which is a beautiful example of repentance with restitution. *"And Zacchaeus stood and said to the Lord, "Behold, Lord, the half of my goods I give to the poor. And if I have defrauded anyone of anything, I restore it fourfold." And Jesus said to him, "Today salvation has come to this house, since he also is a son of Abraham." "For the Son of Man came to seek and to save the lost."*

The words *to seek and save the lost* **rang in my ears. If you are not lost you don't need the Chart Book. If you are not a sinner you don't need a Savior. Just then I heard the crewman say that the only good Christian is a dead Christian! I pondered that statement and asked him to explain further. He said that a man cannot be born again into the Kingdom of God unless he is dead! To be born again means that we have to die first to self before we can be born-again. The crewman told me that many people want to be born again without dying to the self-life and those things in this world that they hold so dear. He told me that a man must turn from the old life if he's to receive new life in Christ. Death of the old man and repentance must precede**

conversion. He said that God hates mixture. The new wine must be put into new wineskins. And man must leave father, mother, and close family relationships to follow Jesus. Death of close relationships is often the hardest thing to give up, but the hope of a new life in Christ is what God wants for us, and so others may see the wonderful transformation that is produced by the new life in Christ. We cannot follow Christ, still clinging to anything or any relationship that would distract us from complete dedication to our Lord. It is all or nothing without any bargaining or compromise.

> *"And brother will deliver brother over to death, and the father his child, and children will rise against parents and have them put to death. And you will be hated by all for my name's sake. But the one who endures to the end will be saved."* (Mark 13:12-13)

I commented to the crewmen that I never heard the gospel message of Christ put that way before. He replied that truth pierces our heart and can be painful. The message to give up all and follow Christ has never been popular, but nevertheless true. Man wants salvation without cost or cheap grace. Costly grace is that which cost Christ everything, in that he died on the cross for our sins, and also requires his disciples to pay the cost of turning from the world and all its distractions to focus on Christ. Christ promises to allow trials and tribulations to come to his disciples, but also promises never to forsake or leave them. Jesus said in John 15:20 : *"A servant is not greater than his master. If they persecuted me, they will also persecute you."* **And Hebrews 13:5-6:** "I will never leave you nor forsake you." **So we can confidently say,** "The Lord is my helper; I will not fear; what can man do to me?"

Christ promises to give us the Holy Spirit as a teacher, advocate, enabler, and guide. Jesus promised to see us through all the storms but never promised that there would not be any storms. Our

25

ship, the 3T, appears ugly to the unsaved that do not want to pay the ultimate price of death to self. It is a ship of beauty to those that are being saved or have been saved and have counted the cost of walking with our Savior. Maybe, he said, the ship should be called the 4T, since truth was interwoven with tribulation, trials, and troubles. Perhaps it's the truth of the cost of discipleship that is most unattractive to those who mock our ship. The crew went on to say that our ship would never be large or attractive but it's a ship that will make it through the storms and over the shoals ahead to reach its destination of the Promised Land and Heaven beyond where our Master is waiting.

I remember the Scripture were Paul says he dies daily. I thought, how can I die once and say that I am crucified with Christ yet still have to die daily? They explained that we die only to what we know is an impediment to our walk with God or an idol. We've died to our known sins and the power of sin has been broken. When we come to Christ we still have the proclivity to sin. While sin no longer has power over us, we still must die daily to the temptation of sin. While we no longer are under the power of sin, we have that same sin nature that must be brought to the cross daily. We'd all like to have a once and for all type of salvation, where not only is the process complete, but we're no longer tempted by sin and we can walk the perfect upright life thereafter. We don't want to deal with our sin nature again and again. Unfortunately, our sanctification is a continuous process that requires continuous vigilance. The wonderful news of God is that Christ purchased the effective grace for our salvation once and for all on the cross and then said, *"it is finished"* (John 19:30). The price was paid in His blood on the cross forever, yet our sin nature must constantly be subdued as we run the race of our life to the ultimate end of bringing glory to God.

We must be careful to remember that Christianity is about bringing glory to Christ, the Father, and the Holy Spirit. Man and his need for salvation are important, but the center of Christianity is about the Glory of God. *"To them God chose to make known how great among the Gentiles are the riches of the glory of this mystery, which is Christ in you, the hope of glory."*(Col. 1:27)

>"And we all, with unveiled face, beholding the
>glory of the Lord, are being transformed into the
>same image from one degree of glory to another.
>For this comes from the Lord who is the Spirit." (2
>Cor. 3:18)

The purpose of salvation is to bring death to our old man so that the new man might behold the Glory of God and show the Glory of God in this world and the world to come. God is the center of all being and the universe; not man. The emphasis is not being **saved from** hell but being **saved unto** Christ, that we might glorify Him. Man floats in the sea of life grasping at possible life preservers until he recognizes the certainty of death and hell. He is often more interested in saving himself rather than glorifying God. Such a man will be disappointed since kingdom living in heaven is all about glorifying God and not man. Such men seek amiss looking to be **saved from** damnation and eternal suffering rather being **saved unto** a new life in Christ. These men will never come to the Kingdom of God or see God's Glory.

When given a choice, man would rather save himself by some type of works that bring glory to himself, rather than to be justified by faith alone. False religions bring men into captivity by offering salvation by some type of works! How we fallen men would gladly accept a salvation that could be earned rather than received as a free gift from our Savior. That is because we want the glory of our salvation for ourselves rather than God.

Just at that moment, one of the crewmen told me to look aside and I saw an old Mississippi River paddle wheeler from the late 1800s paddling in the sea called "Earn your Way into Heaven." This one had large glass windows and I could see that men and women were walking on a series of treadmills, which were attached by belts and a series of pulleys to the paddle wheels. They seemed quite happy, but I felt sad that they much preferred to earn their salvation and power of their own boat by their good works than to rely on God. They didn't seem to notice that this riverboat was unsuitable for the rough seas ahead.

They did not seem concerned that salvation was not earned by works but by grace. They never thought that if man can add something of value to deserve his salvation then this would rob God of His glory and Christ died in vain. It implies that Christ's sacrificial work on the cross was inadequate. If man could add his works to the finished work of Christ, then Christ misspoke when He said, *"It is finished!"* (John 19:30) That would make God a liar and God cannot lie! These men didn't realize that nothing could be added to the *perfect work* of Christ on the cross. Those that would try and add their works to the works of Christ blaspheme God and their ships like this Mississippi paddle wheeler will flounder in the rough seas ahead and all will drown.

As we sailed closer to the Promised Land I began to see more ships in our area. There were three classes of ships. One was man-centered, another was church-centered, and a small number were God-centered. All the ships were headed in the same general direction, but when troubles, storms, whirlpools and other dangers occurred I feared that the ships, which were either man or church-centered, would be lost. It seems so ironic that a ship that was church-centered could be lost. It seems so subtle how the focus in many churches is on serving the church and doing things for the church instead of God. The church takes precedence and subtly draws all of man's time and attention away from the centrality of Christ. Many churches are in direct competition with Christ for adoration. My heart mourned for the ships and they were filled with many good people who wanted to serve the Lord, but were trapped in a ship that was certain to flounder.

The man-centered ships could not navigate in the storms and through the rocky shoals because their focus was on trying to please everyone. It was not possible to choose the best course without offending someone.

The church-centered ships were also unable to navigate successfully through the reefs and shoals because the clergy had a tight control over the rudder of the ship and would not yield to the leadership of the Holy Spirit. Their focus was to maintain their church control even when they lost their direction. The people on the ship had hoped to find salvation through teaching and obedience to the Church officials such as Popes, Cardinals, Bishops, pastors, and other church leaders. Church doctrine and tradition had become equal to and often greater authority than the Bible itself. Church leaders have taught that if you believe and follow Church doctrines and church leadership you will find God, salvation, and ultimately go to heaven. The people were told that God had approved of their church doctrines, leadership, liturgy, and church traditions. Many were told that if they were baptized, they were saved.

Many believed God in their head, but were never told about believing God in their heart or given the message of the whole gospel. Some had sat in the same pew for more than thirty years but never found what their function and purpose was in the church. They simply sat and listened to the sermon and then went home wondering, "Surely church had to be more than this." Church professionalism robs many of the opportunity to serve, since professional staffers have replaced them. The call to discipleship is not just about teaching basic doctrine, but helping people find and operate in their spiritual gifting. Feeding the sheep is much more than giving spiritual food via good biblical preaching. To feed means to promote the spiritual welfare, to nourish, as well as cherish. It is leading the sheep to good pasture where they can grow by learning their proper place of ministry in the flock.

> "Simon, son of John, do you love me more than
> these?" He said to him, "Yes, Lord; you know that
> I love you." He said to him, "Feed my lambs." He
> said to him a second time, "Simon, son of John,
> do you love me?" He said to him, "Yes, Lord; you
> know that I love you." He said to him, "Tend my
> sheep." (John 21:15-16)

Every man is called to be part of the kingdom of priests. When churchmen operate in their correct priestly role, it often causes conflict and competition with the clergy who often forget that their role is to serve the sheep and help each sheep be positioned in their proper place of service.

> *"To him who loves us and has freed us from our*
> *sins by his blood and made us a kingdom, priests*
> *to his God and Father, to him be glory and domin-*
> *ion forever and ever."* (Rev. 1:5-6)

Many are leaving their churches, not because they are unrepentant unbelievers, but because they want more of God. They are looking for more meaningful, transparent fellowship where they can express themselves and grow with others. Fortunately, many of those that got out of the church boat and cast themselves into the sea to form small groups would be swept by the waves to the Promised Land.

Reformed doctrine has been that regeneration or being "Born Again" precedes conversion. The time required for the regenerative process to be completed may take minutes or many years. We are saved by grace and it is grace of God that brings us through the repentance/conversion process. Repentance and conversion are two different sides of a coin and cannot be separated. Many evangelicals teach that repentance follows conversion in that we are saved by grace alone without requiring repentance! A call to be "Born Again" without repentance seriously misrepresents the gospel and produces nothing more than carnal Christianity and antinomianism. Antinomianism means "against the law." If we are saved by grace alone then I can't lose my salvation, therefore we don't have to obey the law; do we, and then why repent? Free grace also encourages a gnostic world view meaning that if the material world and the flesh are corrupt and evil then I will just trust in Jesus and wait for Him to deliver me or rapture me out of this world.

God's standard of confession followed by true repentance is not only costly but an anathema to secularists. Evangelical leaders, who desire Orthodox Christianity, are increasingly being marginalized by liberal humanists. Unfortunately too many evangelical leaders, in an effort to gain cultural leadership and acceptance, minimize the offense of the cross. They preach "Free Grace" rather than costly grace. They desire acceptance and the praise of men rather than endure the ridicule of secular cultural leaders! They promote self-esteem and narcissism.

Western man is focused on a religion of narcissism, which answers the question "what is in it for me?" The call to give up all, to die to self, and follow the Lord is diametrically opposed to todays self centered culture and the message of the postmodern church; "you can have it all, you are special, God wants to bless you and God loves you just the way you are!" Western entitlement mentality is also reflected in, and may be largely a consequence of the message preached by many churches that God owes you blessing because He is a good God and wants to promote your self-esteem. God want you to be rich and drive a nice car! This is a religious entitlement message that encourages a false sense of self worth, narcissism, increasing government demands to provide "what is rightfully owed us," redistribution of wealth, and eventually culminates in socialism. We don't believe in "costly grace" but believe in a lie, "cheap grace." We must humble ourselves, pray, confess, and repent of our personal self-centered agenda, entitlement mentality, and selfishness and lay it at the foot of the cross; then say "Lord, have your way with me, no matter what the cost!"

> *"If my people who are called by my name **humble** themselves, and **pray** and **seek** my face and **turn** (repentance) from their wicked ways, then I will hear from heaven and will forgive their sin and heal their land." (II Chronicles 7:14)*

Chapter 4

FALSE COMFORT AND FALSE HOPE

My head was spinning at all the events of the evening. I went down below and had a cup of coffee with another one of the crewmen. What godly men were sailing the ship. I expressed my concern and pain, because I had seen so many people drowning because they rejected the truth. Conviction of the truth and wisdom of God and His Word cannot save man if it is just intellectual assent. This is just a head-trip. Saving knowledge must be in the heart. A man who is convinced of the truth of the Gospel in his intellect can be persuaded to change his mind by a persuasive argument or evidence. A man who believes in his heart can never change his heart knowledge since it is based on a spiritual witness and not on an intellectual argument. Heart knowledge believes when all the pressures of this world would suggest otherwise. Once a man is convinced in his heart, a man's faith will stand any challenge, tribulation, torture, or torment. Heart faith will not fail when challenged by some teacher who disputes and questions the truth of Scripture. A man who knows God understands the veracity of Holy Scripture. Heart faith is a gift of God by the work of the Holy Spirit to the undeserving repentant sinner. Therefore no man can boast in his faith since it is a pure unearned gift from God!

Non-regenerative man may see the benefits of Christianity. **Unsaved man wants God's power, promises, prosperity, and presence; but not the Lordship of God's Person.** Man wants the benefits of Christianity without paying the cost and carrying the cross or losing control of his life. Man would prefer to have fire insurance rather than life assurance. The non-regenerative man believes that if he throws a few dollars in the offering plate and attends church regularly, then his fire insurance is a paid-up policy. His view of heaven is that it's an endless party where he will celebrate his salvation with all his friends and relatives. Un-regenerative man wants to be the center of all things and hopes to be the center of all things in heaven. He believes God created all things for man's pleasure rather than to show God's glory.

Man by nature is an idolater. He idolizes those that have "made it." He admires successful people in business, athletic pursuits, and people of great beauty and talent such as movie stars. He admires people who are "at the top of their game." The carnal man wants the good life and expects God to provide it.

God is a jealous God and a Holy God. He does not tolerate spiritual adultery. If God is not the center of a man's life then He is not God at all. Most men are worshiping some other type of god such as the god of prosperity, popularity, and the praise of men. Often men preach a god of salvation without cost saying, "Only believe in Jesus and you will be saved." The true gospel is "give up everything and follow Jesus, our savior, and 'Master Mariner.'" We are to leave all personal relationships, business ties, and anything that entangles us with the things of this world and follow Jesus.

"Do not think that I have come to bring peace to the earth. I have not come to bring peace, but a sword. For I have come to set a man against his father, and a daughter against her mother, and a daughter-in-law against her mother-in-law. And a person's enemies will be those of his own household. Whoever loves father or mother more than me is not worthy of me, and whoever loves son or daughter more than me is not worthy of me. And whoever does not take his cross and follow me is not worthy of me. Whoever finds his life

will lose it, and whoever loses his life for my sake will find it." (Matt. 10:34-39)

The Christian life is really an exchange from the old life to the new life in Christ. It is like running a race. When we run; we strip ourselves of our old clothing and put on the new clothing of the righteousness that is in Christ. We run a race where many false finish lines make us think we've arrived and then quit. We soon forget that the race is a lifetime event and the race is not completed until we are at death's door. We're to run with endurance by the provision and power of the Holy Spirit, without wavering, as we pass through difficult trials, temptations, and tribulations. (2 Timothy 4:6-8)

The race is more like a steeplechase than a straightforward race around a well-groomed track in the sunlight with many in the grandstands applauding. The steeplechase has many obstacles to jump over resulting in many falls associated with cuts and bruises. It is very long and fatiguing. The race runs through woods, swamps, and deserts where there are dangerous snakes and animals. The race is often lonely and there is no one to applaud when we successfully negotiate an obstacle. Sometimes it seems that nobody cares and nobody sees our struggles. During the race there are mockers and tormentors who throw stones at us and mock us. We sometimes look at ourselves fatigued and covered in blood and mud and wonder if it is worth it. The race runs through the night, which makes it very difficult to see where we are going and avoid danger. We trip and fall many times but get up and continue the race set before us. We try and remember that eventually the race will end and we will see the rising Morning Star. We will see our God.

" Not that I have already obtained this or am already perfect, but I press on to make it my own, because Christ Jesus has made me his own. Brothers, I do not consider that I have made it my own. But one thing I do: forgetting what lies behind and straining forward to what lies ahead, I press on toward the goal for the prize of the upward call of God in Christ Jesus." (Philippians 3:12-14)

The purpose of God for man is to show His glory. Heaven is about the Glory of God and only those that are seeking the Glory of God will be there. The apostle Paul said in Galatians 2:20:

"I am crucified with Christ. It is no longer I who live but Christ in me, and the life which I now live in the flesh, I live by faith in the Son of God, who loved me and gave himself for me." Later, Paul states in Galatians 6:14: *"God forbid that I should boast except in the cross of our Lord Jesus Christ by whom the world has been crucified to me and I to the world."*

Jesus said to his disciples in John 15:20: *"that the servant was not greater than his master, if they persecuted me they will persecute you."*

True discipleship is costly and the carnal man seeks to avoid the cost and the cross, yet seeks to gain heaven! This spiritual man understands that the process is going to be painful and still seeks to be changed and challenged daily, no matter what the cost.

Our discussion was interrupted via cries for help. We reached out and pulled aboard another man floating aimlessly in the sea who'd come from a ship called *"The False Comfort"* also from Laodicea, Turkey. This man had accidently fallen overboard and he praised the ship and said the people were very kind and loving as well as sympathetic. They had reached out to all those that were lost at sea. Their leaders called out, "God didn't do it" when speaking of shipwrecks, storms, disasters as well as his own unfortunate accident. He then went on to explain that God was a good God and would never do anything to injure or allow righteous people to suffer or die. I immediately thought that if God didn't do it, who surely did?

Religious people would say, "The Devil did it," which often is a subtle way of indirectly blaming God. And who made the Devil? If the Devil did it then they are saying that God is not in control of the affairs of men because He can't control Satin; therefore God allowed this to happen. This means that God is only sovereign if He doesn't allow suffering or evil! Many people ask: "Why do the righteous suffer or why does God allow bad things to happen to good people?" This is of course the wrong question. The biblical question is, "Why does God allow good things to happen to evil people?" We all deserve God's judgment yet he shows mercy!

Scripture is very clear that God is sovereign in everything and nothing can happen in Heaven or on earth without God's permissive will. There is no limit to his authority; it is universal and complete!

"But our God is in the heavens: he hath done whatsoever he hath pleased." (Ps. 115:3) He "works all things after the counsel of his own will." (Eph. 1:11) "Of Him, and through Him, and to Him are all things: to whom be glory forever. Amen." (Rom. 11:36)

God is sovereign and is the creator of all things. He allows wars, troubles, natural disasters, persecutions, as well as world financial collapse. He punishes the wicked and disciplines his children, the elect.

"I form light and create darkness, I make well-being (peace and prosperity) and create calamity,

I am the Lord, who does all these things." (Isa. 45:6)

False comfort says peace, peace, when there is no peace. False comfort implies that God ignores our evil ways! True comfort speaks of the righteous judgments of God and warns of the soon coming judgment of this world for its unrighteousness. True comfort conforms to the righteous plans of God, which men already know in their hearts. God will not be mocked and He hates evil.

"Your throne, O God, is forever and ever, the scepter of upright-ness is the scepter of your kingdom. You have loved righteousness and hated wickedness"; Hebrews 1:8-9

"Hate evil, and love good, and establish justice in the gate"; Amos 5:15 *"For you are not a God who delights in wickedness; evil may not dwell with you.*

The boastful shall not stand before your eyes; you hate all evil-doers." Psalm 5:4-5

He sees the corruption of this world and he is preparing his punishment for the wicked. The righteous are comforted by knowing that God sees the extent of the wickedness of this world and are then comforted by the certainty of His judgment. It is comforting to know that God's kingdom will come and the wicked will be pun-ished and God will bring a new heaven and new earth. There is no need to understand why the righteous suffers and the wicked go unpunished on earth when we understand that God's ways are perfect in all his dealings with men.

Those of little faith question why He allows evil. They believe they'll be comforted if they could understand the ways of God. They have assured themselves that if they have answers to difficult questions about good and evil that they will find peace for their souls. God in his Word has said He works all things for good and works all things for His glory. (Rom. 8:28-39; 9:21-23) That statement is sufficient for me and should be sufficient for the believer whose trust is in the character of God. The questions about having to know the ways of God, speak of the fleshly lust to obtain knowledge of God, which satisfies the flesh rather than the spirit. Saving faith is about trusting God and not about understanding God. The spiritual man understands the goodness of God and His righteousness. He has faith in the character of God and knows that everything He does is perfect and that the suffering that He allows in this world is for His purpose and for His glory.

After listening to this man from *"The False Comfort,"* in frustration I told him to quit his wining, moaning, and complaining, for the King who is faithful and true is coming to judge the earth and restore righteousness! He is looking for those with true faith on earth. Remember that those Israelites who complained in the desert never made it to the Promised Land. After my rebuke the man jumped back in the sea and swam back to "The False Comfort."

Two other ships came into view also from the Laodicean Religious Cruise line. They were the ships of *False Hope and False Assurance.* They had four decks. The top deck of *The False Hope* was called the Universalism Deck. Here the leaders assured everyone that they would be saved. The next deck was the believers' deck and this was reserved for all those who believed that the Master Mariner was the Son of God. They acknowledged him as a historical figure but did not have a living dynamic relationship with him. The lower deck was for good people that felt they were good enough to get into paradise. The lowest deck

was for those that were baptized members of a religious group that believes that the master was a great teacher and that the chart book was a great book of wisdom. Everyone seemed very happy and content.

The sister ship called *False Assurance* had on the top deck all right-thinking people. Here were people who trusted in their theology and knowledge of things of God. They trusted in religious knowledge to get them to paradise. The middle deck was called *False Repentance*. These people had turned from their sin in their heads, but not in their hearts. They still lusted after various sins but did not practice them. The next lowest deck was called *No Cost and No Suffering*. They claimed their God was a good God and would not allow the righteous to suffer. Right belief and faith should protect the believer from suffering hardships and poverty. The bottom deck was called *Church Practice*. It was for those believers that felt they would be saved because they were members of the best church in the community. It was salvation by association.

I mourned as I saw the ships pass by. The mate on our ship said our message hadn't changed for 2,000 years. It was a message of grace alone through faith alone. We were thought not to be culturally relevant and obviously not successful.

Another ship of the Seeker Sensitive Cruise Line passed by called the *Purpose Driven Cruise Ship* from Southern California. These people were purpose driven and mission oriented. Their purpose was to help people find their human potential through the knowledge of God. They emphasized peace and justice and tried to build faith in people. They had a dream and they would help others find their dream. They believed that they could build hope and purpose in man. They had a new reformation and a new spirituality. Their success was evident by a large number of disciples that crammed their ships. They were seeker friendly. They tried to be careful to follow the chart book, but I was afraid they would lose their way and run aground because they disdained the ancient paths. They had invented "New Paths." They were going to change history with their "Global Peace Plan."

Their teaching of the "immanence within" or that God is within every man is also the teaching of prominent New Age authors. Their focus on finding self-esteem is the focus of pop psychology and is not Christian. Jesus came not to save or reform self, but to slay the self. If we die to self, we will find our true selves in Christ. We are to become Christ-centered and not self-centered. The purpose of the church is not to empower men, but to empower Christ through us.

Many of these people had a real passion for the lost, but unfortunately had difficulty in dealing with some of the hard truths in God's Word about predestination, original sin, total depravity, limited atonement, and the sovereignty of God. Somehow they believed that the world needed a better message and a better messenger!

They didn't have a very good knowledge of history. They seemed to have forgotten that for centuries people had tried to change the gospel message to make it more palatable, but this had been unsuccessful. History has taught us that Biblical Christianity has never been popular. It has been estimated that far less than 10 percent of the Roman Empire was Christian at the time of Christianity's greatest spiritual victory over Roman pantheism with the declaration of the Edict of Milan by Constantine in 313AD. This edict formally accepted Christianity and forbade further persecution of the church in the Roman Empire. Under Constantine's leadership pagan temples were converted into churches and pagan priests became Christian priests bringing with them many pagan practices and vestments. The government supported priests, making Christian leadership profitable and dissension very costly. Constantine continued his own worship of the Roman sun god until he was baptized on his deathbed. It was not long after Rome's acceptance of Christianity that the quick rise in the pre-eminence of Christianity morphed into the dark ages and a dark formal religious system with syncretism and many pagan overtones. Christianity paid a huge cost by becoming the state religion, not only by the power of the Emperor, but also by being seeker sensitive and incorporating many pagan practices into the church to make it culturally acceptable.

Soft peddling and compromising the gospel never works. Very few want to hear a message, *come and die and find a new life in Christ.* They don't seem to understand that they were warned at the end of the Chart Book (Bible) that anybody who added to or took away anything from the Chart Book would lose his place in the holy city.

The desire to "win souls" has been the justification of secular marketing techniques and strategies to a consumer based "what is in it for me?" culture. Religion has become a commodity to be marketed, in a user-friendly pattern to a secular, confused, needs based, self-centered culture looking for meaning in life. The message is very subtlety anti-biblical and not Christian! Man is no longer a hopeless sinner, in need of the only Savior, Jesus Christ, and without any ability to help himself without the grace of God. Instead, there are many paths toward god and the releasing human potential. The message morphs into finding *the god within* rather than finding *the God without!*

The seeker sensitive message is about finding self rather than losing self. It is about self-fulfillment rather than self-denial. It is about reformation rather than death to self and rebirth in Christ. It is about forgiveness without repentance. It is about believing that you are a good person, not facing eternal damnation, and that God needs you and wants to use you and your gifts. The truth is we are hopeless sinners with nothing to give God and facing eternal damnation. It is by God's grace that we are saved, and by His grace that we are used for His eternal purposes. We are not chosen because of our own merit or talents. Remember, God used twelve largely ignorant men, fishermen and a tax collector to change the world!

"Then Jesus told his disciples, "If anyone would come after me, let him deny himself and take up his cross and follow me. For whoever would save his life will lose it, but whoever loses his life for my sake will find it." (Matt. 16:24-25)

Just as these ships passed by I saw another giant Texas sized ship approaching us called the *USS Enterprise* from the Religious Cruise Line based in Laodicea. It was followed by a

fleet of smaller "seeker sensitive" ships that were also hoping to learn how to be successful in growing such a large wealthy ship. The ship was over 1,000 feet long. It was twenty stories high. I thought it would be impossible for a ship of this size to make it through some of the narrows and shoals to get to the Promised Land. The ship approached the shallows but had to stop because of its size and chose to remain in the shallows. The leaders were worldly wise and had studied their audience carefully. They did extensive marketing research to find peoples' needs and then orient the church to needs based teaching and sermons. They were pragmatic like many Americans. They thought they could make church work. It was consumer driven or seeker sensitive.

They were non-confrontational with no call for true repentance and death to the old man. They had many different programs thinking that they could capture more people for the church with diversification of programs. Soon the many programs ran the church. Most people seemed happy on the ship. They had their bowling group, 12-step program that focused on reformation rather than rebirth, Bible studies focused on self-help rather than self-sacrifice, softball team that encouraged fellowship without accountability, and it seemed like an endless list of activities and meetings for every age group. The head pastor was like a CEO of a large multi-million dollar corporation with a large salary and a lot of business savvy and money raising skills.

The leader's sermons were clever and humorous but not deep, and were full of Christian platitudes. His sermons were devoted to self-help, man-centered issues, successful living, and building self-esteem rather than expository teaching and doctrinal issues found in Scripture and church creeds. The sermons were more entertainment than enlightenment. The pastor assumed he had God's approval and blessing because of his large number of followers. Some people met the Master Mariner on this ship, but gradually became dissatisfied with cruising the shallows and sought deeper water.

The head pastor was careful not to offend. He was more of a manager of a large enterprise than a broker of truth. Church leaders may try to be deep and speak of the way of the cross, but it does not change anybody unless they are living it. An old pundit once said, "What you are speaks so loud, I can't hear what you say." The message and the life lived must match.

The leadership avoided controversial issues such as abortion and homosexuality. They avoided being accused of hate speech or confronting government officials. They hid behind "the separation of church and state" to preserve their US Tax Code 501-C3 Tax Exempt status as a non-profit church or charity. Financial security was more important than being salt and light to a fallen world. If the church doesn't confront wickedness, how are the sheep going to stand for righteousness? If we Christians are silent, passive, and compromising, we have no right to complain about the invasion of evil in our land. Christians are called to be warriors, not groveling wimps! Where is the outrage about the moral decline of Western civilization? The evangelical church is largely silent!

Evidently the leaders thought it was better to stay in the shallows than take the risk of going around in uncharted waters. The people were very complacent and did not appear to be interested in venturing away from their present position. They were satisfied with their life and wealth. They enjoyed the music and good food and there was lots of entertainment. There was activity for all ages including a climbing wall, a gym, many swimming pools and areas for lots of games. There was also a great choice of upscale restaurants. "Self-indulgence" and "Gluttony" were the names over some of the fine restaurants that featured an endless buffet of the finest cuisine.

I couldn't help but to think of the words of Jeremiah the Prophet who warned about compromise. The financial success of big churches attracts leaders and church followers greedy for gain. They seem willing to compromise the hard truths of Scripture to maintain their financial and church leadership positions.

"For from the least to the greatest of them, every-one is greedy for unjust gain; and from prophet to priest, everyone deals falsely. They have healed the wound of my people lightly, saying, 'Peace, peace,' when there is no peace." (Jer. 6:13-14)

I have thought that if the great tidal wave was ever to come against this ship that it would flip over quickly and all would be lost. Evidently there were some on board that heard from an angel of coming doom and judgment from God, but they were mocked and laughed at by the crew and passengers. These small groups took to the lifeboats, which held about twelve to twenty people. They decided to risk all, including family, friends, money, approval by society, and promotion, to try and make it to the Promised Land on their own. The captain told them they would never make it without pastoral leadership and control. He had great difficulty releasing the lifeboats. He thought that it was necessary to have at least one pastor in every lifeboat that was accountable to him as a spiritual leader. These people had no hope in themselves, but they had hope in the Master Mariner as their leader and that by His spirit, He would guide them through the wind and tides, and over the shoals into the Promised Land.

Chapter 5

WORD OF FAITH

It wasn't very long before I heard another voice crying, "Help!" I saw a man struggling in the water and threw a life ring to him and pulled him aboard. He told me he came from the great ship "*Word of Faith.*" The ship was the largest and most elegant ship of the Prosperity Cruise Line. The ship had gold plated bathroom fixtures and gold plated railings throughout. There was a flag flying over the stern that said, "*Name it and Claim it and Blame it or Blab it.*" No expense was spared in building the ship. The leaders said that nothing is too good for God's children. They and the crew were impeccably dressed in their finest clothes. The leaders emphasized that poverty was simply a problem of the mind. With the right confession any man could become rich. Life was just a big candy store to those who knew the New Testament secret of getting riches! I thought that these leaders were most interesting and I asked nicely for what scriptural evidence they had for this health and wealth prosperity gospel. After listening to him I could not find any scriptural foundation for his theology. This made this group a cult or pseudo-Christian because they denied many of the essential doctrines of historic Christianity. They supported their views by telling us many testimonials of people that had been healed and made rich by following the precepts of their movement. I explained to him that Satan would use any type of deception such as gold

dust, filling people's teeth with gold fillings, slaying people in the spirit, or miraculous healing if this would bring people into deception and bondage to a lie. He explained to me that one of the secrets of their success was the *"principle of giving to get."* **"We're sowing seed by financially supporting their ministries." They explained that God says** *"ask of me what ever you want and I will do it for you."* **I retorted that to ask anything in Jesus' name is to ask in Jesus' character and according to His will. In the book of First John, our Lord speaks through 1 John 5:14-15 and says:** *"<u>If we ask anything according to His will</u> He hears us. And if we know that He hears us in whatever we ask, we know that we have the request that we asked for."* **Prayerful petitions to God begin with submission to His will, as the Lord taught us to pray in the Lord's prayer, and desire that** *"His will be done in heaven and on earth."*

They believed that everything that happens to us is the direct result of our words, using texts like Mark 11:22-25, Luke 6:37-38, Psalm 37:4, and Philippians 4:19.

Have faith in God. Truly, I say to you, whoever says to this mountain, 'Be taken up and thrown into the sea,' and does not doubt in his heart, but believes that what he says will come to pass, it will be done for him. Therefore I tell you, whatever you ask in prayer, believe that you have received it, and it will be yours. And whenever you stand praying, forgive, if you have anything against anyone, so that your Father also who is in heaven may forgive you your tres-passes." (Mark 11:22-25) Notice the context of these verses. They are about forgiveness and not obtaining wealth!

> *"Be merciful, even as your Father is merciful. Judge not, and you will not be judged; condemn not, and you will not be condemned; forgive, and you will be forgiven; give, and it will be given to you. Good measure, pressed down, shaken together, running over, will be put into your lap. For with the measure you use it will be measured back to you."* (Luke 6:37-38)

Please notice the context is about being merciful, not judgmental or unforgiving. It is not about giving money in order to receive money. The message that our Lord wants us to understand from that verse is that we will receive God's mercy and forgiveness as we give mercy and forgiveness to others. The verse is not about money, but about forgiveness. In hermeneutics or the rules of biblical interpretation, context is king.

They were taught that words are spiritual containers and that the force of faith is released by words such as in Psalm 37:4: *"Delight yourself in the Lord, and he will give you the desires of your heart."* Philippians 4:19 states: *"And my God will supply every need of yours according to his riches in glory in Christ Jesus."* It is our faith filled words or "positive confession" that are creative in the universe today according to their teaching. We have what we ask if what we ask is according to God's will for us. Man becomes in charge of providence rather than God. Man forms his own destiny to find "Health, Wealth, and Success." Their leaders are "Proof Texting" or taking various Scriptures out of context to support their teaching. This is very deceptive. All Scriptures must be judged by the whole context of the Bible. Jesus also says:

> *"But woe to you who are rich, for you have received your consolation."*
> *"Woe to you who are full now, for you shall be hungry."*
>
> *"Woe to you who laugh now, for you shall mourn and weep."*
> *"Woe to you, when all people speak well of you, for so their fathers did to the false prophets."* (Luke 6:24-26)

"How difficult it is for those who have wealth to enter the kingdom of God! For it is easier for a camel to go through the eye of a needle than for a rich person to enter the kingdom of God." Those who heard it said, *"Then who can be saved?"* But he said, *"What is*

impossible with men is possible with God." And Peter said, "See, we have left our homes and followed you." And he said to them, "Truly, I say to you, there is no one who has left house or wife or brothers or parents or children, for the sake of the kingdom of God, who will not receive many times more in this time, and in the age to come eternal life." (Luke 18:24-30)

Riches in the Kingdom of God are spiritual and obtained by righteous living, obedience, and sacrifice.

> *"Rejoice in the Lord always; again I will say, Rejoice. Let your reasonableness be known to everyone. The Lord is at hand; do not be anxious about anything, but in everything by prayer and supplication with thanksgiving let your requests be made known to God. And the peace of God, which surpasses all understanding, will guard your hearts and your minds in Christ Jesus."* (Phil. 4:4-7)

There is such a wonderful peace when you give to the Lord all the burdens and desires of your heart and you can rest in the sovereignty of God. We make our requests known to God knowing in Romans 8:28 that *"He works all things for good."* How I praise the Lord for the many things I requested but He didn't allow because He had a better plan. God wants to give us His best, not our best.

We ask amiss whenever we ask for things that are not in God's will for us. For many wealth is a curse and the things of this world distract us from the things of God.

In the Book of Proverbs, Chapter 30, Agur prays: *"Two things I ask of you: deny them not to me before I die. Remove far from me falsehood and lying: **give me neither poverty nor riches**: feed me with the food that is needful for me, lest I be full and deny you and say 'Who is the Lord?' or be poor and steal and profane the name of my God."*

Jesus reminds us in His sermon on the mount: *"Do not lay up for yourselves treasures on earth, where moth and rust destroy and where thieves break in and steal, but lay up for yourselves treasures in heaven, where neither moth nor rust destroys and where thieves do not break in and steal. For where your treasure is, there your heart will be also"* (Matt. 6:19-21).

I couldn't believe how arrogant these men were who had deified man and believed that man was a little god who could create things by his word. In actuality, these leaders were really teaching a type of Christian witchcraft using certain prayer and faith techniques to conjure or call certain things into existence. These faith leaders were taking into their own hands human prerogatives that belong to God alone. The root of this deception is in an occult metaphysics and pantheism, which proclaims the divinity of man. Subtly God has become the servant of man, rather than man becoming the servant of God. I could see that this man was very sincere, but confused and would not receive correction. Many people arrived on the ship by helicopter. Many of the passengers had given all they had to buy a ticket aboard this prosperity ship. They knew they were going someplace as the ship cruised in circles going nowhere.

These "word of faith" leaders have led many people astray, particularly the poor, the weak, and the ignorant with a false prosperity gospel. This lie from Satan attracts people because of their greed and lust for the things of this world. Peter tells us that:

"False prophets also arose among the people, just as there will be false teachers among you, who will secretly bring in destructive heresies, even denying the Master who bought them, bringing upon themselves swift destruction. And many will follow their sensuality, and because of them the way of truth will be blasphemed. And in their greed they will exploit you with false words. Their condemnation from long ago is not idle, and their destruction is not asleep" (2 Pet. 2:1-3). And in verses 14-15 of chapter two, Peter goes on to say: *"They have hearts trained in greed. Accursed children! Forsaking the right way, they have gone astray. They have followed the way of Balaam, the son of Beor, who loved gain from wrongdoing,"*

Paul warns us in 1 Timothy 6:6-10 about the consequences of covetousness, envy, and greed. *"Now there is great gain in godliness* with contentment, for we brought nothing into the world, and we cannot take anything out of the world. But if we have food and clothing, with these we will be content. But those who desire to be rich fall into temptation, into a snare, into many senseless and harmful desires that plunge people into ruin and destruction. For the love of money is a root of all kinds of evils."

I asked this man how he ended up in the sea. He told me that when they discovered his poverty and lack of success in life, they damned him for unbelief and called him a bad example for others on the ship, so they threw him overboard. I told him that I had hoped that a dip in the cold water would have sobered him up from the deceptive teaching and had brought him to reconsider the error of his ways. I could see that God had a plan to deliver him. He began shaking and crying and we all prayed that he would be freed from his deception. What we couldn't do by trying to correct his theology, God could do in a few minutes through the work of the Holy Spirit. With time he repented and was restored to his right mind. He asked if he could remain on the ship and we gladly accepted him.

Chapter 6

SITUATIONAL ESCHATOLOGY

I saw another ship approaching over the Horizon. It was a large imposing ship called The *"Rapture"* from the Dispensational cruise line. The crew told me that the ship had representatives of all the major evangelical denominations on board. The ship looked like an aircraft carrier because it had a long flight deck crowded with people at ease sitting in lawn chairs, dressed in summer casual clothes sipping drinks, waiting for the return of Jesus. The people were not dressed for the coming storms because they felt Jesus would return for them and rapture them to heaven ahead of any storms, trials, or tribulations that lie ahead. They seemed very happy and I was amazed at their confidence in the soon coming of Jesus. Whenever a large wave would rock the ship, everyone would look up to the sky. I asked the crewman to explain to me what the biblical foundation for their beliefs was?

Eschatology, from Greek *eschatos* or last, is the study of the last things or end times. Christians have had four major views of end time events; amillennialism, postmillennialism, historic premillennialism and dispensational premillennialism. Dispensationalism is a recent popular Protestant evangelical tradition and theology based on a new biblical hermeneutic, or a literal system of interpretation, that sees a series of chronologically successive 'dispensations' or periods in history in which God relates to human beings in different ways under different biblical covenants. As a system dispensationalism is rooted in the writings of John Nelson Darby and the Brethren Movement beginning around 1830. The theology of dispensationalism consists of a distinctive eschatological 'end times' perspective, as all dispensationalists hold to premillennialism meaning 'before the millennium' and most hold to a "pre-tribulation rapture."

"Hold it," I said, "you are using too many big words for me."

Let me explain, he said: "Basically the dispensationalists believe that Jesus is going to return to establish a millennial kingdom on earth for 1,000 years after a period of great tribulation lasting seven years. They believe in two comings of Jesus. The first is called the rapture, at which time only the church will be removed. This could occur at any moment. They believe that the church is composed of those, and only those that are saved between Pentecost and the rapture. After the rapture the Jewish remnant will be God's agent on earth. Most dispensationalists think this rapture would occur before the great tribulation. This is called pretribulation rapture.

Dispensationalists believe there will be a second coming of Jesus with the saints at the time of the defeat of Satan at the end of the millennial period. In the meantime, after the church has been removed; the Jewish remnant will be empowered by the Holy Spirit for the conversion of the remaining unsaved Gentiles to begin the millennium."

Dispensationalists believe that the nation of Israel is distinct from the Church and that God will fulfill His promises to national Israel. These promises include the land promises, temple promises, and Jewish worship promises, which in the future result in a millennial kingdom where Christ, upon His return, will rule the world from Jerusalem for 1,000 years. Dispensationalists believe God has two distinct programs for history, one for Israel and one for the church. The church does not take over any of Israel's promises or purposes. The church age is thought of by dispensationalists as a 'parenthesis or intercalation' or a period of time when God has temporarily suspended His primary purpose for Israel. The church age begins at Pentecost and ends at the pre-tribulation rapture of the church. The Jewish saints such as Abraham, Joseph, Moses and others will not be part of the rapture of the church! After the rapture of the church, God continues His promises to redeem Israel and the Jewish Saints.

The concept that the church is just a "parenthesis" conflicts with Scripture. Paul makes it very clear in his epistles that the Old Testament points to the coming of Christ whose sole purpose and ultimate goal is to build his church, Jews and gentiles, which is now and ever more will be the temple of the Holy Spirit. (Romans 9-11) The church is not a replacement of the Jews (Replacement Theology) but is grafted into the rootstock of the olive tree of Israel. The promises of God are inextricably intertwined together with Jew and gentile. (Romans 11) All the true Israel, (Galatians 3:13-29) the promised seed of Abraham, who believe by faith will be saved. (Romans 11:26)

> *"And he put all things under his feet and gave him as head over all things to the church, which is his body, the fullness of him who fills all in all."* (Eph. 1:22-23)

> *"So that through the church the manifold wisdom of God might now be made known to the rulers and authorities in the heavenly places. This was according to the eternal purpose that he has realized in Christ Jesus our Lord, in whom we have boldness and access with confidence through our faith in him."* (Eph. 3:10-12)

> *"Husbands, love your wives, as Christ loved the church and gave himself up for her, that he might sanctify her, having cleansed her by the washing of water with the word, so that he might present the church to himself in splendor, without spot or wrinkle or any such thing, that she might be holy and without blemish."* (Eph. 5:25-27)

Dispensational premillennialism needs to be distinguished from Historic Premillennialism, which is also called Chiliasm (Greek, chilioi for one thousand) or Millenarianism (Latin mille for one thousand), which was often the view of many of the saints in the early church, particularly during periods of great persecution and the appearance of many antichrist like world leaders. They looked forward to the soon return of Christ in their generation at the end of their present tribulation to establish His millennial kingdom on earth for 1,000 years. This theological perspective did not include the rapture or a special dispensation for Israel. Examples are Hippolytus (170-236) and Sextus Julius Africanus (160-240) who taught the world would end around 500 AD. The later Fathers also stood firm in the conviction that there would be a final judgment at the end of the world. They spoke of this mostly, just as of other eschatological events, in a highly rhetorical fashion, without conveying any definite information. Augustine assumes that the scriptural representations of end times are figurative. He expresses the conviction that Christ is coming again to judge the living and the dead.

The rise of Islam brought much speculation about the emergence of the antichrist and the soon return of Jesus. Followers of Jan Hus thought that the return of Christ would come in 1420. Martin Luther (1483-1546) thought that the return of Christ would occur in the next hundred years. Cotton Mather (1663-1728) predicted the end of the age would be 1736. Jonathan Edwards (1703-1758) predicted the final return of Christ around the year 2000. William Miller predicted the return of Christ in 1843 then changed it to 1844 when Christ did not return as expected in 1843. More recently Hal Lindsey and Edgar Whisenant predicted the return of Christ in 1988. Recently there has been speculation about the return of Christ in 2012! It is best not to speculate about Christ's return in the future but live each day as if He would return tomorrow!

In other areas of theology, dispensationalists hold to a wide range of beliefs within the evangelical and fundamentalist spectrum. It is important to recognize that good Christians have argued amongst themselves for the last 2,000 years about the nature of the millennium. There has been no consensus among theologians about the millennium. There has been however, a general consensus among Christian theologians for 1,800 years about the single return of Christ for all believers, Christian and Jew, until Darby's speculation in 1830 of a pre-tribulation rapture of the church only, followed by a second coming of Christ at the end of the millennium for Israel and those converted during the millennial period.

The disagreement between various denominational and theological camps of the proper interpretation of the concept of a rapture is presented in 1 Thessalonians 4:17.

1 Thessalonians 4:13-18:

"But we do not want you to be uninformed, brothers, about those who are asleep, *that you may not grieve as others do who have no hope. For since we believe that Jesus died and rose again, even so, through Jesus, God will bring with him those who have fallen asleep. For this we declare to you by a word from the Lord that we who are alive, who are left until the coming of the Lord, will not precede those who have fallen asleep. For the Lord himself will descend from heaven with a cry of command, with the voice of an archangel, and with the sound of the trumpet of God. And the dead in Christ will rise first. **Then we who are alive, who are left, will be caught up together with them in the clouds to meet the Lord in the air,** and so we will always be with the Lord. Therefore encourage one another with these words.*"

How did this teaching of the apostle Paul ever come to be called the Rapture? The answer lies in the word translated "shall be caught up" (Greek *harpagésómetha* from verb *harparzo*). In Latin, this word is *rapere* or *rapio*, as used in the Latin Vulgate translation of the Bible, from which the English word "rapture" is derived. Free of any arcane or mysterious interpretation, it simply means "to be caught up," "snatched," or "seized."

Dispensationalists place their emphasis on the Greek word *harparzo* translated, "to be caught up" or raptured. Other non-dispensationalists place their emphasis on the word "to meet or meeting" or *apantesis* from the Greek *apantáo* from *apó* = from + *antáo* = to come opposite to, to meet especially, to meet face to face. It describes a meeting, especially a meeting of two who are coming from different directions. In Greek culture the word had a technical meaning to describe the visits of dignitaries to cities where the visitor would be formally met by the citizens, or a deputation of them, who had gone out from the city for this purpose and would then be ceremonially escorted back into the city. *Apantesis* was often used to suggest the meeting of a dignitary, king, or famous person, describing people rushing to meet the one who was coming.

In Hellenistic Greek, the expression had become a kind of technical term denoting "a ceremonial meeting with a person of position." In papyrus usage it was used of an official delegation going forth to meet a newly appointed magistrate, or other dignitary, upon his arrival in their district. Greek scholars Hogg and Vine have commented that, *"Almost invariably the word suggests that those who go out to meet him intend to return to their starting place with the person met."* In other words, the purpose of those Christians who meet Jesus in the air is not to be taken away with Him but to escort Him to His throne where He will rule and reign over the earth!

The same Greek word *apantesis* is used in Acts 28 to describe the meeting of Paul with the saints in Rome. They came out of the city to meet Paul and they escorted him into the city of Rome.

*"And so we came to Rome. And the brothers there, when they heard about us, came as far as the Forum of Appius and Three Taverns to **meet** us. On seeing them, Paul thanked God and took courage."* (Acts 28:14-15)

The concept of an *apantesis* today is still the correct protocol to bring a dignitary into a city. In the United States a foreign dignitary is always met at Andrews Air Force Base by State Department, White House dignitaries, and military officers and then escorted into Washington D.C. A Roman General returning from a conquest was made to wait outside of the city for three days so that the city could make appropriate preparations and then the City Officials would come out and meet the dignitary and lead him into the city. Jesus will meet his church in the air as victorious Lord and King for the sole purpose of having the Church take Him to His throne, where we will rule and reign with Him.

The proper interpretation of 1 Thessalonians 4:16-17 is that at the end of time Jesus is going to be seated on His throne on the New Earth or New Jerusalem with his Church to rule and reign forever. Jesus returns only once to earth and not twice! He is coming, not to get His Church out of trouble or tribulation, but in His perfect time He returns to be enthroned with His Church to rule and reign forever. There is no secret rapture but Christ openly displaces Himself!

The dispensationalists' interpretation is that the rapture is about escape from tribulation and removing the church from a great time of Satan's anger, which has caused great tribulation and great persecution of the church. This coming world wide chaos and woe implies that God is unable to protect His church during the time of tribulation and that Satan's power on earth is temporarily greater than Christ's who eventually becomes victorious. Think about that! Scripture is very clear that the "Prince of this World" can do nothing that is not under God's control. Satan has already been defeated at the cross. The church through the work of Christ on the cross is victorious NOW as well as later!

"He disarmed the rulers and authorities and put them to open shame, by triumphing over them in him." (Col. 2:15)

Why is this so important? Many want to escape troubles and trials. The concept of a rapture or deliverance out of a fallen world on the verge of collapse is very attractive to many. However, this results in an attitude of apathy, passivity, and laziness about the things of the Lord. Why improve or busy yourself about the Lord's business, if He is coming soon and is going to get us out of our financial and relational troubles? Basically, the belief in the rapture of the church from certain destruction produces apathy, escapism, and a weakened church.

Dispensational thinking encourages many Christians to retreat from society rather than being salt and light to a fallen generation. Moral is critical for a victorious church. If Satan can convince many that the Antichrist is coming to rule and reign soon, then this produces spiritual paralysis, fear, and a weakened church. Victorious Christianity needs a positive eschatology to stand and fight in these difficult times. Christ has left great power to His church that it may rule victoriously.

> *"Believe me that I am in the Father and the Father is in me, or else believe on account of the works themselves. "Truly, truly, I say to you, whoever believes in me will also do the works that I do; and greater works than these will he do, because I am going to the Father. Whatever you ask in my name, this I will do, that the Father may be glorified in the Son. If you ask me anything in my name, I will do it." (John 14:11-14)*

> *"For though we walk in the flesh, we are not waging war according to the flesh. For the weapons of our warfare are not of the flesh but have divine power to destroy strongholds. We destroy arguments and every lofty opinion raised against the knowledge of God, and take every thought captive to obey Christ, being ready to punish every disobedience, when your obedience is complete." (2 Cor. 10:3-6)*

Proverbs 22:13 speaks to the issue of sloth and fear, which is epidemic in the church: *"The sluggard says, "There is a lion outside! I shall be killed in the streets!"* This can be paraphrased as: *Satan, the roaring lion is outside in the streets and so I am going to stay inside of my house (church) and wait for God to rapture me out of here.*

Instead be a warrior, an overcomer, battling Satan in the streets and taking territory back from him, rather than like many who are hiding in their closets! How sad!

We need to remember the teaching that the Church would be raptured to heaven leaving a Jewish remnant behind, just prior to a time called the great tribulation, was not known prior to the 1830s. Dispensationalists admit that this is a relatively new theology unknown to the ancients. Historical premillennial non-dispensational eschatology was believed by some of the early church fathers that looked forward to the final coming (*Greek parousia: coming or appearance*) of Jesus to establish His eternal Kingdom. The historic premillennial worldview sees the Bible as a history of the Jews and the church from beginning of time to the final coming of Christ. There is no special rapture of the church first and then later the Jews. Historic premillennialists believe that the Jews will be saved during end time events and raptured together with other Christians. The traditional understanding was that there was only one coming of the Lord who would return for his church, Jew and gentile, and then rule and reign for an indefinite millennial period with His church. The doctrinal statement in the Apostles' Creed precludes a premillennial advent of Christ or two comings.

The debate among many Christians is about the millennial period. Does the millennium or 1,000-year period mentioned in Revelation chapter 20 mean a literal 1,000-year time period or is this a metaphor for spiritual warfare? Amillennialists believe that we are now living in the millennium, which began at Pentecost. Postmillennialists believe in the gradual expansion of the Kingdom of God until a victorious Christ returns. The church was not to be removed from earth but would meet (*apantesis*) Jesus in the sky and escort Him to His throne to rule and reign with Him on earth.

The traditional view of the mainline denominations and the view of the reformers and Augustine is amillennialism. The amillennial view holds that the 1,000 years mentioned in Revelation chapter 20:4-6 is a symbolic number, not a literal description; and that the millennium has already begun and is identical with the current church age, (or that it ended with the destruction of Jerusalem in AD 70, which is the view of preterists). Amillennialism holds that while Christ's reign during the millennium is spiritual in nature, at the end of the church age, Christ will return in final judgment and establish a permanent physical reign on earth. Revelation 20:4–6 is the chief and nearly the sole support of the doctrine of two corporeal resurrections. It is very dangerous to build a major church doctrine around one Bible verse. Remember that neither the phrase *second resurrection* nor the phrase *first death* is found in Scripture. Christ comes twice. First to the Jews as portrayed in the gospels, and again He returns again for His Bride in First Thessalonians 4:17. The first and only resurrection occurred in the gospels. Christ returns again after the first resurrection for all the saints in Revelation 20:9-15. They are inferences from the phrases *first resurrection* and *second death*, the former in Rev. 20:5–7; the latter in 2:11; 20:6, 14; 21:8. One death and one resurrection are directly taught, and only one death and one resurrection followed by one final return of Christ are directly taught in Scripture.

The concept of a literal 1,000-year millennial period misinterprets a prophetic expression meant to express a long period of unknown duration. God doesn't think of things in the context of time, since he exists outside of time. He created the universe and the earth outside of time or before time began. Time didn't begin until God created the first day with light and darkness. God cannot be defined by time since He existed before time and is timeless or eternal. The concept of eternity means that it is a period not definable by the measure of time. God has His plan, which cannot be defined by man's literal mechanistic concept of time but will be defined by God Himself.

It is inconceivable that the Church could have endured through the centuries without some voice being raised in support of the current premillennial dispensational doctrine, if it does have any validity. Since no ancient voice spoke out in favor of this doctrine, the only conclusion possible is that the Church did not teach this in the beginning, and it should not be teaching it now. It is very dangerous to form a major doctrine on one verse or particularly one word in that verse!

More importantly, the dispensational pessimistic worldview that things are going to get worse and worse until Jesus raptures His church to save it from the great tribulation demeans God! It makes God appear to be powerless against His vanquished foe Satan. Satan's war against the Saints of God has become so effective that the only way God can save His church is to rapture it out of the clutches of Satan to heaven! Please, this is terribly pessimistic and unbiblical theology! We are called to be warriors and overcomers and to defeat our vanquished foe. We are called to be victors and not victims!

> *"Yours, O Lord, is the greatness and the power and the glory and the victory and the majesty, for all that is in the heavens and in the earth is yours. Yours is the kingdom, O Lord, and you are exalted as head above all." (1 Chron. 29:11)*

> *"Beat your plowshares into swords, and your pruning hooks into spears; let the weak say, "I am a warrior." (Joel 3:10)*

> *"For everyone who has been born of God overcomes the world. And this is the victory that has overcome the world— our faith." (1 John 5:4)*

> *"Behold, I have given you authority to tread on serpents and scorpions, and over all the power of the enemy, and nothing shall hurt you." (Luke 10:19)*

> *"I have said these things to you, that in me you may have peace. In the world you will have tribulation. But take heart; I have overcome the world." (John 16:33)*

> *"I write to you, fathers, because you know him who is from the beginning. I write to you, young men, because you are strong, and the word of God abides in you, and you have overcome the evil one." (1 John 2:14)*

We are more than victors in Christ and need not fear man or Satan. *"No, in all these things we are more than conquerors through him who loved us. For I am sure that neither death nor life, nor angels nor rulers, nor things present nor things to come, nor powers, nor* height nor depth, nor anything else in all creation, will be able to separate us from the love of God in Christ Jesus our Lord." (Rom. 8:37-39)

Our eschatology (Doctrine of end times) shapes our Ecclesiology (Doctrine of the Church) and our Christology (Doctrine of Christ) as well as our Soteriology (Doctrine of salvation). Sound doctrine produces a stable, growing, productive spiritual life. Defective doctrine produces weak Christians and a weak Church. The belief in a weak Christ with a weak helpless Church in an overwhelmingly strong evil world system of Satan results in a completely distorted view of the victorious Christ and the victory we have through Him. Weak Christians live in fear of the coming antichrist and the tribulation rather than in victory. Christians are called to expand the Kingdom of God, to raid the enemy's camp, and to take prisoners for Christ. Those who live in fear and hide in their houses will be *Left Behind*! We are called to subdue and take dominion over the earth.

> *"And God said to them, "Be fruitful and multiply and fill the earth and subdue it and have dominion over the fish of the sea and over the birds of the heavens and over every living thing that moves on the earth." (Gen. 1:28)*

Remember what Jesus did on the cross: *"He disarmed the rulers and authorities and put them to open shame, by triumphing over them in him,"* (Col. 2:15).

Those critics of my anti-dispensational worldview might think that I support radical "Dominion Theology," "Kingdom Now Theology," "Latter Rain Movement," "The New Apostolic Reformation," and" The New Paradigm" theologies which purpose a progressive revelation of Christ resulting in worldwide evangelism and perfection of His Bride, the church through the release of end time anointing of a "new group" of Apostles and Prophets. Many of the current self-appointed apostolic leaders are very elitist and plan a global international movement to take over churches and nations. These men appear to be more interested in fleecing the flock rather than equipping the saints as in Ephesians 4:11-12. The church needs men of vision and true leaders who are humble servants and not pride filled self-centered narcissistic men or women who claim special revelation and anointing from God to manipulate the saints. These leaders believe Christ will then return to rule with his church, only after the earthly rule has been established by these self-appointed apostles. Scripture warns us "*But it is not the spiritual that is first but the natural, and then the spiritual.*" (1st Corinthians 15:46). The false precedes the true. Today's apostolic, prophetic ministry is but a shadow of the release of the Holy Spirit to come. God is raising up humble anointed men to equip and edify the saints who will not to draw men to themselves but focus men on Christ. (Ephesians 4:11-13)

Many postmillennialists hope that God's law will be the basis for all rule and behavior (theonomy). The Kingdom of God or a "Christian Republic" will be established on Earth through political and (in some cases) even military means as opposed to the work of the Holy Spirit.

Some postmillennialists have adapted a type of social gospel focused on "social justice" and have focused on eradication of various vices such as slavery, alcoholism, child labor, prostitution, and other social evils and inequalities. Reconstructionists hope to renew society by demanding observance to God's moral law and seek to change society by applying biblical moral standards. Their focus is not only on personal discipleship and salvation, but the discipleship of nations through the transforming power of the Holy Spirit. Their motive is laudable but there is a very fine line between the works of man and the work of the Holy Spirit!

Traditional postmillennialism visualizes a less radical and more gradual world change as the gospel is spread throughout the world until the gospel is preached unto the ends of the earth. The transformation of man is the end result of a work of the Holy Spirit and not the result of mans' institutions. This results in the millennial return of Christ who then will establish His rule on earth.

Postmillennialism is very positive and hopeful, when it is the work of the Holy Spirit, but has been distorted by some who believe that Jesus will not return until his earthly Kingdom has been established by these very dangerous self-appointed "apostles and prophets" who want control of the church for their own selfish purposes. This demonic doctrine of "A New Apostolic Reformation" is a work of man rather than a work of God and is not new.

Martin Luther said: "*One must not make out of this the kind of kingdom or seek the sort of church that may be governed on earth by external secular power. The pope does this and praises it as the true church government. The Anabaptists and similar erring spirits dream that before the Last Day all the enemies of the church will be physically exterminated and a church assembled which shall consist of pious Christians only; they will govern in peace, without any opposition or attack. But this text clearly and powerfully says that there are to be enemies continuously as long as this Christ reigns on earth. And certain it is, too, that death will not be abolished until the Last Day, when all His enemies will be exterminated with one blow.* (Luther's Works Vol. 13:263-264)

John Calvin expressed the view of many of the reformation scholars in his comments on 1st Thessalonians 4:17: "*And so we shall be ever. To those who have been once gathered to Christ he promises eternal life with him, by which statements the reveries of Origen and of the Chiliasts are abundantly refuted. For the life of believers, when they have once been gathered into one kingdom, will have no end any more than Christ's. Now, to assign to Christ a thousand years, so that he would afterwards cease to reign, were too horrible to be made mention of. Those, however, fall into this absurdity who limit the life of believers to a thousand years, for they must live with Christ as long as Christ himself will exist. We must observe also what he says—we shall be, for he means that we profitably entertain a hope of eternal life, only when we hope that it has been expressly appointed for us.*" Calvin's Commentaries on the Epistles of Paul; 1st Thessalonians 4:16-17).

The reformers understood that Christian hope could be replaced by a hope in the return of Christ to set the world aright (**Christ as savior**) rather than a hope in Him alone (**Christ as Lord**); a very subtle, but important distinction.

Many Christians today hold an intermediate view, which I call **Situational Eschatology,** which means what I believe about end times is largely shaped by current world events and what I read or see on television, or the Internet, about the world situation. Our understanding of end times or eschatology is too often shaped largely by current events and despair about the world situation rather than the positive view of Scripture. This has been a problem in the church from the first century and the destruction of Jerusalem in 70 AD. Evil rulers such as Nero and other despots, the fall of nations such as the fall of Rome in 410 AD, the rise of Islam, the plagues that killed as many as one-quarter to one-third of the European population in the middle ages, wars such as the Hundred Years War, and natural disasters such as the great earth quake that destroyed Lisbon in 1755, signs in the sky such as comets, eclipses, all produced an outcry that this was certainly the end of the world. Many thought that with the appearance of Haley's comet in 989 that Christ would return in the year 1,000. The Taborites were radical followers of Jan Hus and predicted the return of Christ in 1420. Augustine and Martin Luther felt they were living in the last days. Cotton Mather, the great American Puritan pastor, (1663-1728) thought Christ would return in 1697 and then later changed the date to 1736. Jonathan Edwards predicted the return of Christ in the year 2000! Hal Lindsey predicted the return of Christ in 1988. The re-establishment of the Nation of Israel in 1948 and capture of the temple mount in 1967 has further stoked end time speculations that Christ would return in that generation of forty years (1988 and 2007). This did not happen so new speculations have followed about the year 2012!

Fear and pessimism saps the church of its vitality and ardor. We claim to believe Scripture that Jesus and the Kingdom of God will triumph, but often feel overwhelmed by the seemingly great victory of evil in this wicked world. Unfortunately, at this time in church history, eschatological or end time teachings of the return of Christ are often far more important to the evangelical church than His ethical precepts!

The amillennial view, as well as the dispensational premillennial view, can be rather pessimistic when it focuses on the here and now rather than our blessed hope. Pessimism produces fear, fatalism, and what is even worse, immobilization! Amillennialists recognize the evil in this world system (I John 5:19) but at the same time expect a total renewal of God's creation with the return of Christ. (Isaiah 65:17-25) The amillennialist sees God at work in his Kingdom now and looks forward to its future consummation. When we look at the world we quickly forget that Satan has been defeated at the cross and is the vanquished foe. No matter how bad things look socially and politically, Christians are called to stand and fight for righteousness and societal transformation. We are the "*salt of the earth.*" We are victors and not victims.

> *"Finally, be strong in the Lord and in the strength of his might. Put on the whole armor of God, that you may be able to stand against the schemes of the devil. For we do not wrestle against flesh and blood, but against the rulers, against the authorities, against the cosmic powers over this present darkness, against the spiritual forces of evil in the heavenly places."* (Eph. 6:10-12)

Much of the confusion in Christendom today also relates to our understanding of our initial resting place before Christ returns from Heaven to rule and reign. Many of the Saints now believe that Christians go directly to heaven, as did Darby and the early nineteenth century revivalists who popularized the concept that Christians go directly to heaven bypassing the intermediate state.

For the first 1,800 or so years since the resurrection of Jesus, Christians have believed that the departed go to an intermediate place called paradise like the thief on the cross. (Paradise: a royal park or garden, Luke 23:43, 2 Cor.12:4, Rev 2:7 as opposed to heaven a transcendent kingdom where God and angels dwell and the final destination of the elect.)

Paradise is a state of conscious existence in the presence of our Lord and not "soul sleep." There we will await the final return of Christ in Paradise to rule and reign with Him forever. (Psalms 16:10, 49:14-15, Ecc 12:7, Luke 16:22-43, Phil 1:23, 2 Cor 5:8, Rev 6:9-11, 14:13) I think of Paradise as a temporary place where we will be learning more about our Lord in preparation of His return and our rule with Him. The ancients understood that death is just a transition from our mortal life to a new spiritual life where we will be transformed into the likeness of Christ. Jesus said, *"If anyone keeps my word, he will never see death."* (John 8:51; 5:24-25) The biblical concept of death is eternal separation from God, not cessation of bodily function. The best description for death for the Christian is *transition* or the passing from one life to another. Those who love God will never be separated from Him and in a spiritual sense never die! We will be like Adam and the earth will be restored and God's original plan for earth will be carried out under the rulership of the Second Adam, Christ.

We are to remember that God doesn't change His plans nor can He be defeated. The vision of His ultimate plan for the Garden of Eden and man is outlined in the first three chapters of Genesis and then repeated in the last three chapters of the book of Revelation. Here we see again the tree of life, the garden, and the river, the beginning of history and the end of history. The early church and the reformers understood that all spiritual life is about doing God's business. Heaven is not about sitting on a cloud playing a harp. Kingdom work never ends even in eternity! We will rule and reign with Jesus forever and ever.

I thought about the postmodern church and its false concept of Heaven as a place of just eternal bliss and rest where nothing will be required of the saints other than praise and a grateful heart! Modern man is more concerned about a reunion with loved ones and having an endless party than Kingdom business.

For many postmoderns, the fear of death and eternal punishment has been replaced by universalism, the hope that all men will be saved, or annihilationism, which is the hope that there is no eternal punishment for the wicked or that punishment will last for varying periods of time and then man will be extinguished or annihilated so that there is an end to the suffering of the wicked. Scripture makes it abundantly clear that there can be no separation in the justice of God: some will come to eternal bliss and others to eternal damnation and torment. Jesus spoke more of Hell than Heaven! There are 21 passages in the four gospels where Jesus warns unrepentant sinners about the eternal consequences of sin and eternal punishment in Hell.

> *"Whoever believes in the Son has eternal life; whoever does not obey the Son shall not see life, but the wrath of God remains on him."* (John 3:36)

It is the certainty of eternal judgment, pain and suffering that is the motivating force of evangelism. The gospel is that the condition of the unconverted is that it is as bad as it can possibly be for those who reject Christ. The battle over the doctrine of eternal punishment is a battle over a foundational issue that church creeds and confessions have confirmed as an essential church doctrine as in the book of Hebrews.

> *"Therefore let us leave **the elementary doctrine of Christ** and go on to maturity, not laying again a foundation of repentance from dead works and of faith toward God, and of instruction about washings, the laying on of hands, the resurrection of the dead, and **eternal judgment"**.* (Hebrews 6:1-2)

> *"And just as it is appointed for man to die once, and after that comes judgment, so Christ, having been offered once to bear the sins of many, will appear a second time, not to deal with sin but to save those who are eagerly waiting for him."* (Hebrews 9:27-28)

And these will go away into eternal punishment, but the righteous into eternal life." (Matthew 25:46)

> *"Christ; who suffered for our salvation, descended to the world below, rose again from the dead, ascended into heaven, and sat down at the right hand of the Father to come from thence to judge the quick and the dead, at whose coming all men shall rise again with their bodies, and shall give account for their own deeds.* **And they that have done good will go into life eternal; they that have done evil into eternal fire."** *(Athanasian Creed circa 293-373 AD)*

"The rest of mankind God was pleased, according to the unsearchable counsel of His own will, whereby He extendeth or witholdeth mercy, as He pleaseth, for the glory of His sovereign power over His creatures, to pass by; and to ordain them to dishonour and wrath for their sin, to the praise of His glorious justice." (Matt. 11:25—26, Rom. 9:17—18, 21—22, 2 Tim. 2:19—20, Jude 4, 1 Pet. 2:8) (Westminster Confession of Faith 1643, Chap 3, #7)

"The end of God's appointing this day is for the manifestation of the glory of His mercy, in the eternal salvation of the elect; and of His justice, in the damnation of the reprobate, who are wicked and disobedient. For then shall the righteous go into everlasting life, and receive that fullness of joy and refreshing, which shall come from the presence of the Lord: but the wicked, who know not God, and obey not the Gospel of Jesus Christ, shall be cast into eternal torments, and be punished with everlasting destruction from the presence of the Lord, and from the glory of His power." (Matt. 25:31—46, Rom. 2:5—6, Rom. 9:22—23, Matt. 25:21, Acts 3:19, 2 Thess. 1:7—10) (Westminster Confession of Faith 1643, Chapter 33, #2)

If there is no eternal punishment and eventually all will be saved (universalism) or extinguished (annihilationism), then eschatology is simply unimportant and only an intellectual mind game. We cannot appreciate God's justice, great love, mercy, and the glorious gift of eternal salvation without the contrast of His eternal wrath on the wicked. Eternal punishment motivates evangelism. Paul reminds us that: *"knowing the terror of the Lord we persuade men"* (2nd Corinthians 5:11 NKJV)

Satan has always tried to minimize the consequences of sin and the certainty of eternal damnation of the wicked. The good news is that Satan was defeated at the cross; the bad news is his eternal sentence has not yet been carried out and evil is still with us. God wants us to know heaven now, if we don't know a little of heaven now, how will we know it later? We are new creatures in Christ and need to assume our spiritual authority invading the secular world and take back territory for the Lord. This is our eternal destiny. God's plan never changes. He expects us (new creatures in the Second Adam) to take dominion now and forever.

Unfortunately, many Western Christians have a defeatist worldview that the world is evil, corrupt, and hopeless, which has its roots in Gnosticism and Platonism, which in turn denies the goodness of creation. Salvation then becomes an escape from the world to heaven or the afterlife. When God created this world, animals, and man He said: *"It is good!"* The purpose of salvation is not to get a ticket out of this world or fire insurance from Hell, but life assurance through an ongoing living relationship with Jesus Christ our Lord. The proper focus is in "The Lord's Prayer," *let your kingdom come.* We are to pray for His Kingdom to be manifested now as well as in the future. Creation is not to be cursed but redeemed. *Then God said, "Let us make man in our image, after our likeness. And* **let them have dominion** *over the fish of the sea and over the birds of the heavens and over the livestock and over all the earth and over every creeping thing that creeps on the earth."* (The word rule or take dominion in Hebrew means **râdâh**: *to tread down, have dominion, prevail against, reign, [bear, make to] to rule over, take.*) *"And God blessed them. And God said to them, "Be fruitful and multiply and fill the earth and* **subdue it and have dominion** *over the fish of the sea and over the birds of the heavens and over every living thing that moves on the earth."* (Gen. 1:28) (The Hebrew word here is **kâbash**: *to tread down; to tread under your feet, hence, to disregard; to* conquer, subjugate, violate, bring into bondage, force, keep under, subdue, bring into subjection.)

Both of these Hebrew words speak of taking dominion or ruling over an enemy or that serpent Satan. The first Adam failed but the second Adam succeeded and crushed the enemy's head. God's plan is to prepare the saints to rule and reign with Him by conquering Satan now by living a holy life and taking dominion now over evil at every opportunity.

> *"Therefore, if anyone is in Christ, he is a new creation. The old has passed away; behold, the new has come. All this is from God, who through Christ reconciled us to himself and gave us the ministry of reconciliation; that is, in Christ God was reconciling the world to himself, not counting their trespasses against them, and entrusting to us the message of reconciliation. Therefore, we are ambassadors for Christ, God making his appeal through us. We implore you on behalf of Christ, be reconciled to God. For our sake he made him to be sin who knew no sin, so that in him we might become the righteousness of God."* (2 Cor. 5:17-21)

> *"What then shall we say to these things? If God is for us, who can be against us? He who did not spare his own Son but gave him up for us all, how will he not also with him graciously give us all things?"* (Rom. 8:31-32)

> *"Therefore, as you received Christ Jesus the Lord, so walk in him, rooted and built up in him and established in the faith, just as you were taught, abounding in thanksgiving...for in him the whole fullness of deity dwells bodily, and **you have***

been filled in him, who is the head of all rule and
authority." (Col. 2:6, 7-10)

Modern culture has lost its perspective of history. To the Greek history is about a recurring cycle of events with no culmination and no perfection. To the Hebrew, history has a beginning and an end. It is about a progressive linear history of God's redemptive process culminating in the return of Christ. Hebrew thinking brings meaning to history, since history is progressive; it brings hope and vision for the future. Self-centered Western Christians have seen the promises of Christ's return as an individual hope or privatized eschatology. This further encourages a withdrawal from society and a private piety. Christ is going to return to rule and reign and dramatically change the whole world. He is coming to judge the living and the dead. Justice and righteousness will be established. He is the consummation and the promised goal of all history. **Christ is the purpose of all history and its consummation.** The church is not the goal of history but the tool God is using to prepare and perfect His Bride to meet her Lord and Savior upon His return.

In summary, our Greek thinking, gnostic, narcissistic, and materialistic, society has focused on a **savior from** this world (escapism, dispensationalism) rather than a **savior for** transforming this world and building His kingdom on earth, where He will make us transforming agents to extend His rule and reign! There always will be some eschatological tension between the future and the now. **Our focus need not be on end time events but on being God's agents for societal transformation as salt and light. Maranatha: Come Lord Jesus!**

Chapter 7

THE GOSPEL, JUSTIFICATION, SANCTIFICATION AND A CALL TO HOLINESS

If we understand God's holiness as moral perfection, purity, perfect goodness, and being wholly perfect in every way, so that He is separate and above all things in the entire universe; then we are confronted in the apparent hopelessness of His call for us to be holy like Him. We can only cling to the cross of Jesus and cry mercy, mercy for God is too great for us and we are sinners.

The gospel is the good news of God's redemption of sinful humanity through the life, death, and resurrection of his Son Jesus Christ. Dispensationalism often brings along with its distorted eschatology some very dangerous baggage about soteriology or how man is saved. This relates to the basic understanding of regeneration and antinomianism. In this chapter, I will discuss: 1) What is the proper call for salvation? 2) What is justification? 3) How does sanctification occur?

The major issue in American preaching is related to an evangelical message that promises a quick fix or instant salvation and sanctification at no or little cost or what I call **event** or instant experience based conversion without a call to die to self and begin a life long **process** of progressive sanctification producing holiness. How many face eternal destruction because they were sold instant fire insurance rather than life assurance and a call to progressive holiness?

What is the call to the unsaved but to come and die to give up all and come follow Jesus! God's plan for man is simple but costs everything. Any invitation that is less than a call to radical obedience is unbiblical and compromises the gospel. The biblical message is that the only good Christian is a dead Christian or someone who has died to the old life and the world, and then has been transformed into a new creature in Christ. Holiness is the inward change produced by the indwelling of the Holy Spirit that results in outward behavior pleasing to God and conformable to his commandments. Holiness is produced by death to self.

> *"If anyone would come after me, let him deny himself and take up his cross and follow me. For whoever would save his life will lose it, but whoever loses his life for my sake will find it."* (Matt. 16:24-25)

> *"Do not love the world or the things in the world. If anyone loves the world, the love of the Father is not in him. For all that is in the world—the desires of the flesh and the desires of the eyes and pride in possessions—is not from the Father but is from the world. And the world is passing away along with its desires, but whoever does the will of God abides forever."* (1 John 2:15-17)

> *"Therefore, if anyone is in Christ, he is a new creation. The old has passed away; behold, the new has come."* (2 Cor. 5:17)

The call to holiness can only be understood in the context of our understanding of soteriology or how are we saved. The subject of how we are converted to be servants of Christ and what this means is a daunting task for discussion in any book. The critical issue between reformed or covenantal Christians and dispensationalists is whether conversion changes a person inwardly without an outwardly changed behavior or being a so-called "Carnal Christian." In theological terms this means that there can be justification without sanctification, holiness, or obedience. Obedience is never optional. True saving faith results in submission to the Lordship of Jesus.

> *"For those who live according to the flesh set their minds on the things of the flesh, but those who live according to the Spirit set their minds on the things of the Spirit. For to set the mind on the flesh (carnally minded) is death, but to set the mind on the Spirit is life and peace. For the (carnal) mind that is set on the flesh is hostile to God, for it does not submit to God's law; indeed, it cannot. **Those who are in the flesh cannot please God.**"* (Romans 8:5-8)

Biblical Christians believe that regeneration changes the person inwardly and also outwardly. There can be no such thing as a carnal Christian since genuine faith is a gift of the Holy Spirit and produces a desire to obey our Lord and live in holiness. Furthermore, biblical Christians believe that beginning with conversion we enter the Kingdom of God now and not in the future! Saving faith is the work of the Holy Spirit and changes us to be more conformed into His likeness. (Romans 8:9-14)

> *" You, however, are not in the flesh but in the Spirit, if in fact the Spirit of God dwells in you. **Anyone who does not have the Spirit of Christ does not belong to him.** But if Christ is in you, although the body is dead because of sin, the Spirit is life because of righteousness. If the Spirit of him who raised Jesus from the dead dwells in you, he who raised Christ Jesus from the dead will also give life to your mortal bodies through*

*his Spirit who dwells in you. So then, brothers, we
are debtors, not to the flesh, to live according to
the flesh. For if you live according to the flesh you
will die, but if by the Spirit you put to death the
deeds of the body, you will live. **For all who are
led by the Spirit of God are sons of God.**"*

Some well known evangelical ministries claim: *Receiving Christ
involves turning to God from self (repentance) and trusting Christ
to come into our lives to forgive our sins and to make us what He
wants us to be.* The message is good as far as it goes but does
not distinguish the drawing of the Holy Spirit from the lust of the
flesh, such as individual needs of self-reformation, the need of self
worth, self image, acceptance from others, and fire insurance; all
motivating the choosing of Christ for selfish purposes. Fallen man
lacks understanding of his predicament. We are all sinners without
hope, with nothing to give God other than our humble complete
surrender to God's mercy. To receive Christ by the will of man (man
saves himself) produces a false faith and a false confidence in
Christ as savior and sanctifier. Just to agree intellectually that Jesus
Christ is the Son of God and that He died on the cross for your sins
is not enough. Nor is it enough to have an emotional experience.
When you receive Jesus Christ by faith, as a sovereign act of the
will motivated and empowered by the Holy Spirit, you are called
by the Holy Spirit who will: *" train us to renounce ungodliness and
worldly passions, and to live self-controlled, upright, and godly lives
in the present age, waiting for our blessed hope, the appearing of the
glory of our great God and Savior Jesus Christ, who gave himself
for us to redeem us from all lawlessness and to purify for himself a
people for his own possession who are zealous for good works."* (Titus
2:12-14) There are two circles representing two kinds of lives in the
illustration used in the brochure called "The Four Spiritual Laws."
They are the carnal man who remains on the throne of his life versus
the spiritual man where Christ is on the throne of this person's life.
Man would like to think of himself on the throne by "choosing Jesus."
When Christ chooses us He is on the throne.

75

All Christians believe that we are saved by faith alone but many differ about the "act of the will." This important theological concept came to a head in the fourth century between a British monk named Pelagius who denied original sin and believed in the goodness of man. Opposition came from Augustine who taught that man's will was captive by sin and man could never choose God without regeneration by the Holy Spirit. Pelagians believe that conversion is an act of our own will, while Augustinian Christians believe that they are chosen by God, by His sovereign will, not their will. Those that receive the salvic message of God are those who have been regenerated, or prepared by the Holy Spirit, before converting to Christ. The message of saving faith through grace will only be appropriated by those chosen by God and regenerated by the Holy Spirit. The atonement of Christ is sufficient for all but only efficient for some; His elect.

"And when the Gentiles heard this, they began rejoicing and glorifying the word of the Lord, and **"as many as were appointed to eternal life believed."** (Acts 13:48)

Our hope must be in the sovereignty of God and not in our own wisdom to make the right choice and chose God. Any confidence in our own goodness or cleverness will ultimately lead to deception. Now once saved, how is man justified; by works or grace?

Alister McGrath notes four characteristics of the Protestant doctrine of justification in response to Catholic dogma that were firmly established by the year 1540:

1. Justification is the forensic *declaration* that the Christian is righteous, rather than the process by which he or she is *made* righteous. It involves a change in *status* rather than in *nature.*
2. A deliberate and systematic distinction is made between justification (the external act by which God declares the believer to be righteous) and sanctification or regeneration (the internal process of renewal by the Holy Spirit).
3. Justifying righteousness is the alien righteousness of Christ, imputed to the believer and external to him, not a righ-

76

teousness that is inherent within him, located within him, or in any way belonging to him.

4. Justification takes place *per fidem propter Christum*, with faith being understood as the God-given means of justification and the merits of Christ the God-given foundation of justification.

For Roman Catholics the righteousness of Christ is not *imputed to* the believer, but *infused into* the believer. When the believer cooperates with this infused righteousness (works), the believer then possesses an inherent righteousness, which then becomes the ground of justification.

Luther argued that the righteousness providing the ground of our justification is an "*iustitia alienum*," an "alien righteousness." This is the righteousness of another, one who is a "foreigner" to us. He (Christ) is foreign to us, not in the sense that He is unknown by us or that He remains a mysterious stranger to us, but in the sense that He is ever and always distinguishable from us, even though by faith we are "in" Him and He is "in" us.

Calvin in response to Catholic doctrine concludes with respect to imputation:

> ... "*it is entirely by the intervention of Christ's righteousness that we obtain justification before God. This is equivalent to saying that man is not just in himself, but that the righteousness of Christ is communicated to him by imputation, while he is strictly deserving of punishment. Thus vanishes the absurd dogma, that man is justified by faith, inasmuch as it brings him under the influence of the Spirit of God by whom he is rendered righteous. This is so repugnant to the above doctrine that it can never be reconciled with it.*"

Calvin was distinguishing the salvation by faith alone without trust in the justifying work of the cross, from our justification, which is not a work of man but a sovereign work of Christ for those who have looked to Christ as their savior by faith. Saving faith trusts in the completed work of Christ on the cross and believes that nothing can be added to it such as the catholic view of works of merit. The issue of justification by works versus forensic justification was a critical issue for the reformers and still is a critical issue today. Perhaps this example will clarify the issue.

If your father would give you a great mansion, you might be very grateful until you learn that he only made a down payment and you were required to pay off the principle of $5,000,000 by various works or the bank would foreclose and take the house back from you. This is no different than what is taught by some theologians who suggest that works of merit are necessary to pay off the principle. Indeed, our heavenly father has given us a great mansion, but has completely paid for it by the sacrifice of His Son on the cross. No further payment is needed. When Jesus said, "*It is finished,*" He was affirming that the price of our justification before God was completely paid in full and nothing could be added to it! To diminish the sacrificial completed work of Christ in any way is to diminish God Himself! The believer needs only to gratefully receive his justification by Christ. However, the ability to receive the atoning work of Christ requires the enabling power of the Holy Spirit by the effectual calling of God by His grace!

Thus justification, a declaration of right standing before God, or "just if I never sinned" is not the product of saving faith but saving faith produces trust in, reliance upon, and hope in the already accomplished work of Christ; who purchased our justification for us once and for all at Calvary. Unfortunately, many men would like to justify themselves by works, rather than accept that there can only be forensic justification of God's wrath by Jesus's imputed and sanctifying righteousness purchased for us on the cross.

I saw a vision of a square bed sheet about seven-foot square held tightly upright at each corner by an angel. In the center of the sheet was a round hole just big enough for a man's head to pass through. There was blood sprinkled around the center hole. A man called sinner, wearing black clothing, was stand-

ing underneath the sheet with just his head passing through the center hole. The man was an obvious sinner with spiders, snakes, frogs, dead rats and other types of vermin attached to his clothing. An awful odor oozed from his body. Yet I could see God above looking down from heaven. God could only see the man's head and the covering of the sheet stained with blood that spoke of the righteous work of Christ. God proclaimed that this sinner was righteous and justified by the perfect work and sacrifice of His Son!

Later in another vision I saw this man's dark clothing begin to lighten and the vermin begin to lose the attachment to his body and fall off. He began to loose that offensive smell. I asked the Father what was happening and He explained to me that those He justifies, He sanctifies. If a man will keep his gaze upon Jesus that man will begin to change and slowly his sins will begin to loose their grip on his soul and some would eventually fall away. This work of sanctification stopped when the man took his gaze off of Jesus and looked at others and the world. It began again when he looked up and again placed his gaze and hope in Christ. This work of sanctification would never be complete but a continuous process of change and ongoing work of the Holy Spirit. It was wholly supernatural!

Luther reminds us that we are both justified by the work of Christ yet sinners. (*simul iustus et peccator*) We are both simultaneously Holy before God yet called to be Holy or sanctified. Sanctification reflects God-likeness, purity, and holiness. In Hebrew and Greek it means set apart or to separate. It is the actual transformation in the moral life of the believer that sets him apart. It is a moral turn-around or moral makeover with tangible results. It is like a household complete renovation not simply changing the furniture around. Paul reminds us in Romans 7:12: "*the law is holy, and the commandment is holy and righteous and good.*"

Later in 2 Timothy 2:21-26 Paul again calls Christians to holiness: "*Therefore, if anyone cleanses himself from what is dishonorable, he will be a vessel for honorable use, set apart as holy, useful to the master of the house, ready for every good work. So flee youthful passions and pursue righteousness, faith, love, and peace, along with those who call on the Lord from a pure heart. Have nothing to do with foolish, ignorant controversies; you know that they breed quarrels. And the Lord's servant must not be quarrelsome but kind to everyone, able to teach, patiently enduring evil, correcting his opponents with gentleness. God may perhaps grant them repentance leading to a knowledge of the truth, and they may come to their senses and escape from the snare of the devil, after being captured by him to do his will."*

Again Paul alludes to the constant battle for man's soul. The power to defeat the temptations of this world resides with the power of the Holy Spirit. We are called to an impossible task of personal holiness without the empowerment of the Holy Spirit. The good news is that God didn't set us up for failure but has equipped every believer with power to resist and overcome sin. God has given us His Spirit to cause us to walk after His Holy Laws and obey them!

*"Thus says the Lord God: It is not for your sake, O house of Israel, that I am about to act, but for the sake of my holy name, which you have profaned among the nations to which you came. And I will vindicate the holiness of my great name, which has been profaned among the nations, and which you have profaned among them. And the nations will know that I am the Lord, declares the Lord God, when through you I vindicate my holiness before their eyes. I will take you from the nations and gather you from all the countries and bring you into your own land. I will sprinkle clean water on you, and you shall be clean from all your uncleannesses, and from all your idols I will cleanse you. And I will give you a new heart, and a new spirit I will put within you. **And I will remove the heart of stone from your flesh and give you a heart of flesh. And I will put my Spirit within you, and cause you to walk in my statutes and be careful to obey my rules."*** (Ezek. 36:22-27)

We see this same theme repeated in Ephesians 5:25-27: *"Husbands, love your wives, as Christ loved the church and gave himself up for her, that he might sanctify her, having cleansed her by the washing of water with the word, so that he might present the church* to himself in splendor, without spot or wrinkle or any such thing, that she might be holy and without blemish."

In Hebrews, the author spends most of the first ten chapters explaining our position in Christ and in chapter 12:14 exhorts the reader to remember: **"Strive for peace with everyone, and for the holiness without which no one will see the Lord."**

A man who properly understands his fallen state and the hopelessness of ever meeting God's standard is forced to fall at the feet of Jesus and call for His Holiness to be worked in him. Matthew 5:20 says, *"For I tell you, unless your righteousness exceeds that of the scribes and Pharisees, you will never enter the kingdom of heaven"* and Matthew 5:48: *"You therefore must be perfect, as your heavenly Father is perfect."* Our God is Holy, and cannot see sin. As we seek Him, He will transform us into His likeness. *"But seek first the kingdom of God and his righteousness, and all these things will be added to you."* (Matt. 6:33) It is the grace of God working through the Holy Spirit that changes us into more of his likeness. When we put Him first, the things of this world loose their power over us and fade away. If we lust after the things of this world, we must remember that because of God's holiness that God is offended, since He cannot be separated from his holiness, purity, truth, and justice, which includes the eternal punishment of the wicked. True "Saving Faith," coupled with the knowledge of our own sinfulness, repentance, and the fear of God is what purifies the heart of man and compels him to places his hope in our sanctifier Jesus Christ. We place no hope in ourselves but in Jesus Christ our savior, justifier, and sanctifier. Remember we are not saved by works but are saved for works. (Ephesians 2:10) First John 5:4-5 tells us, **"For everyone who has been born of God overcomes the world. And this is the victory that has overcome the world—our faith. Who is it that overcomes the world except the one who believes that Jesus is the Son of God?"**

Chapter 8

SLOPPY AGAPE

The church today is in crises and confusion over a misunderstanding of God's love. If God is love then He must love everyone including those who are in open rebellion against Him? If God is love then is it wrong to make value judgments on certain moral issues such as homosexuality, abortion, and euthanasia? How can God be a God of wrath, justice, and judgment and still be a loving God? It is this bad theology that has infiltrated various main line denominations resulting not only the approval, but also promotion to church leadership of practicing homosexuals. Hopefully this chapter will help restore a balanced biblical understanding of God's love and man's responsibility.

I was just beginning to feel comfortable when a large four-story ship slowly passed by. The ship had glass walls. It was very easy to see the people at each level in the ship. The boat was called *"The Love Boat"* from Philadelphia, Turkey. The first level ownership was called the *"Storge"* or the love of material things. Here people indulged their love of their material possessions such as boats, cars, planes, animals, hobbies, clothes, houses or any other type of material possession.

The second floor was called *"Eros."* Here man women engaged in erotic sexual activity and the pursuit of such things that please the senses. Eros was erotic sexual love.

The third level of the ship was called *"Phileo,"* or brotherly love. This was a collecting place for people who love each other because of common experiences or other things they held in common such as race, family, social economic status, education, language, place of birth, marriage, and neighborhood residents. Many were from the same church. They genuinely seemed to care for one another but they also formed cliques and often didn't reach out to others who were of different race, socioeconomic status or cultural values.

The fourth and highest level of the ship was called "Agape" or the love of God. This is a New Testament Greek word, not used or understood by Jews or pagans, but only used to describe the very character of God for *"God is love"* (1 John 4:8).

This type of love, agape, was particular only to God. It was a love that man could never obtain for himself but was just the type of love that man is called to steward. This type of love is sacrificial, benevolent, and undefeatable. It desires the highest good for another person. It is unconditional love with unconditional acceptance of another, only if that person has received the righteousness of Christ that was purchased on the cross. It requires obedience and repentance. Jesus tells us "if you love me, you will keep my commandments." This type of love was the essence of God's character and not man's. Man cannot love sacrificially like God in his fallen nature. In fact, fallen man hates God and only loves himself! Consider the sacrifice that God made when He gave his only Son for sinful man and let him suffer and be rejected on the cross so that he could take the sin of man on Himself to be the perfect sacrifice. The magnitude and purity of that love is beyond man's capacity to really even understand let alone practice.

The understanding of God's love begins with the understanding of His Holiness, Wrath and Judgment. "God is light, and in him is no darkness at all." (1 John 1:5) *"Are you not from everlasting, O Lord my God, my Holy One? We shall not die. O Lord, you have ordained them as a judgment, and you, O Rock, have established them for reproof. You who are of purer eyes than to see evil and can-*

not look at wrong," (Hab. 1:12-13) *"God is a righteous judge, and a God who feels indignation every day."* (Ps. 7:11)

> Jesus and the Bible speak more about God's wrath and the future judgment of all men than they speak of God's love! *"The Lord tests the righteous, but his soul hates the wicked and the one who loves violence. Let him rain coals on the wicked; fire and sulfur and a scorching wind shall be the portion of their cup. For the Lord is righteous; he loves righteous deeds;"* (Ps. 11:5-7)

It is only when we grasp the magnitude of His holiness, perfection, and intolerance for wickedness and sin that we can begin to appreciate His love demonstrated through the sacrifice of His Son on the cross for the atonement of our sin!

We have to be very careful how we speak of *agape* love as "God's unconditional love." If God loves me unconditionally does it matter how I live my life? If God's love is unconditional then how can God condemn the wicked? Does unconditional love mean there is no discrimination between good and evil? Does God's love condone evil? If God loves unconditionally then all men will go to heaven and there is no need for evangelism or the church. It is interesting that the term "unconditional love" is not found in Scripture. This false concept of unconditional love is the invention of man and many church leaders who mistakenly believe agape love is unconditional. We frequently hear from the pulpit "God loves everybody!" No! If God loved everyone unconditionally the there would be no need of hell!

One hears frequently that the God of the New Testament, which was written in Greek, is different from the God of the Old Testament, which was written in Hebrew. The words used in Hebrew enlarge upon the New Testament concept of *"agape"* love. Hebrew words such as *"chesed"* or mercy express that God is infinitely and unchangeably good.

> *"The Lord your God is in your midst, a mighty one who will save; He will rejoice over you with gladness; He will quiet you by his love; He will exult over you with loud singing."* (Zeph. 3:17)

His goodness, covenant love, kindness, devotion, mercy, pity, compassion, benevolence, and long-suffering patience are the essence of the Love of God.

> *"The steadfast love of the Lord never ceases; his mercies never come to an end; they are new every morning; great is your faithfulness. "The Lord is my portion," says my soul, "therefore I will hope in him."* (Lam. 3:22-24)

God's gift of repentance and mercy toward a rebellious idolatrous people is seen again and again in the Old Testament. The concept and understanding of God's love is fleshed out in the Old Testament examples of His love of David, Abraham, Joseph, and many others. His mercy and loving kindness is balanced with His wrath and justice throughout all of Scripture. He is the same God with the same love in both the New and Old Testaments. Ephesians 2:4 tell us about God's love and mercy. Mercy means unwarranted restraint of the justice do us because we are all sinners, as opposed to grace, which means unwarranted or undeserved favor from God. We all deserve God's wrath and punishment, but He withholds His just punishment because of His mercy. His mercy is unwarranted but God shows mercy as an expression of His agape love. God is able to show us mercy since His justice was satisfied at the cross as an expression of Christ's sacrificial agape love.

> *"But God, being rich in mercy, because of the great love with which he loved us."* He is incomprehensible by the finite human mind. *"Oh, the depth of the riches and wisdom and knowledge of God! How unsearchable are his judgments and*

how inscrutable his ways! *"For who has known the mind of the Lord, or who has been his counselor?"* (Rom. 11:33-34) We are called to reflect God's love and mercy to a fallen world. *"Blessed are the merciful, for they shall receive mercy."* (Matt. 5:7)

We are told in Scripture to love and show mercy to our enemies but not God's enemies. *"For judgment is without mercy to one who has shown no mercy. Mercy triumphs over judgment."* (James 2:13)

We are told not to associate with the wicked. First Corinthians 5:9-13 says, *"I wrote to you in my letter not to associate with sexually immoral people not at all meaning the sexually immoral of this world, or the greedy and swindlers, or idolaters, since then you would need to go out of the world. But now I am writing to you not to associate with anyone who bears the name of brother if he is guilty of sexual immorality or greed, or is an idolater, reviler, drunkard, or swindler—not even to eat with such a one. For what have I to do with judging outsiders? Is it not those inside the church whom you are to judge? God judges those outside. "Purge the evil person from among you."*

Paul scolded the Corinthian Church in chapter 5 for failure to judge sin in the church, yet in Romans chapter 14 he scolds the church for passing judgment on each other! *"Why do you pass judgment on your brother? Or you, why do you despise your brother? For we will all stand before the judgment seat of God."* (Rom. 14:10) In Romans 14, Paul was dealing with some legalistic Christians who where judging others for eating food sacrificed to idols. We are not to judge others based on their religious practices but still discern and judge major sin in the church. God is the judge of those outside of the church. It is faith working through love that is the foundation of justice and without justice there can be no effective government.

There is no such thing as unconditional forgiveness. Forgiveness is always conditional on true repentance, which includes changed behavior and restitution whenever possible. God's love for us is conditional on our receiving the sacrificial merit of Christ's suffering, confession of our hopelessness without Christ, and true repentance.

> *"If your brother sins, rebuke him, and if he repents, forgive him,"* (Luke 17:3)

It seems so ironic that Scripture calls man to love his brother with the same love that God showed through the sacrifice of His Son and be kind and loving to our neighbor. The command to love my neighbor is the verb form of *agape* love. It literally means to be loving or kind like the example of the Good Samaritan in Luke 10:29-37. We are called to be loving and kind to all, even our enemies, but this is very different from the *agape* love we are to show our spiritual brothers and sisters. Notice we are not called to like or necessarily approve of our neighbor but to show kindness and be loving! We demonstrate our love for God and our neighbor by our obedience to God's commandments.

> *"Owe no one anything, except to love each other, for the one who loves another has fulfilled the law. For the commandments, "You shall not commit adultery, You shall not murder, You shall not steal, You shall not covet," and any other command-ment, are summed up in this word: "You shall love your neighbor as yourself." Love does no wrong to a neighbor; therefore love is the fulfilling of the law."* (Rom. 13:8-10)

Once we understand the difference between God's love, or *agape* love, and our love for one another called *phileo* or brotherly love, we recognize the impossibility of ever loving like God. I fell on my face when confronted with my own selfishness. I knew that I could never exhibit that benevolent, sacrificial love that only belongs to God. This was freeing for me because I began to understand that

God wants to love through me, and that my sin has been the failure to let God have His way in my life and release His love to others. I know that as I have grown in my love for God; I have grown in my ability to love my neighbor. My vertical relationship with God has produced the flow of His love horizontally. It all begins with His love for me, and my love for Him. The more I know of His love, the more of that *agape* love flows from me to my neighbor.

God wants to reach the world through each believer and extend His sacrificial love to many. My problem has been I've been very judgmental and I have said to God, "you can't love this person or that group etc." *Agape* love requires man to die to himself, so God can love whom He wants through us. When I examine myself I understand the hopelessness of trying to emulate Him and His love. The Holy Spirit in me is able to release His agape love through me in a way I could never do myself. My love is very conditional and very performance-based. You perform for me and I will love you. If you don't perform the way I expect, then I will withhold my love from you. God's love is also performance based; fortunately Christ's work on the cross vicariously paid the price for man's sins. It is this work of Christ that allows us to come before God through saving faith and repentance to receive forgiveness and His love. The criteria for meeting performance standards of God were satisfied on the cross that appeased God's wrath. To believe that God's love is unconditional is without biblical foundation! It is conditional through justification by faith in Christ alone. Jesus performed the ultimate sacrificial love because He satisfied God's wrath, judgments, and conditions against mankind through His blood sacrifice. *"For God so loved the world, that he gave his only Son, that whoever believes in him should not perish but have eternal life. For God did not send his Son into the world to condemn the world, but in order that the world might be saved through him. **Whoever believes in him is not condemned, but whoever does not believe is condemned already,** because he has not believed in the name of the only Son of God. And this is the judgment: the light has come into the world, and people loved the darkness rather than the light because their works were evil. For everyone who does wicked things hates the light and does not* come to the light, lest his works should be exposed. But whoever does what is true comes to the light, so that it may be clearly seen that his works have been carried out in God." (John 3:16-21)

John 3:16 is the most often quoted verse in the Bible, but few read any further. God gave His Son for those who would believe but not those who where already condemned and hated the light. God's sacrificial love was poured out only for those who would believe in Him. If God's redemptive work through Christ was for "everyone" then everyone will be saved, which is clearly not the teaching of Scripture.

Mans' love is easily disappointed but God's love is never disappointed. I saw that the only way to resolve the problem was to call on God to love through me. I have attempted in the past to show His *agape* love through the efforts of my flesh but was unsuccessful. I had been getting in the way of God's *agape* love by substituting my *phileo* love for people. Again and again I have had to be reminded that God wants me to get out of the way and He wants to love people and the world around us, even those people I don't approve of! God doesn't try and make me love or like someone with my human *phileo* love. He doesn't ask me to approve of someone. He recognizes that humanly speaking there are some people we like and others we don't. It is not humanly possible to love everybody, but it is heavenly possible! The world doesn't need man's sentimental, gooey, fleshly, performance based, phony, and guilt driven, *phileo* love!

Jesus asked Peter three times in John chapter 21, if he (*agape*) loved Him. Peter responded each time that he (*phileo*) loved Him. Peter knew that he was humanly unable to return that perfect holy *agape* love of Jesus without the power of the Holy Spirit! (John 21:15-17) The empowerment of the Holy Spirit later changed Peter from a fearful recluse hiding in the upper room to a bold warrior for God filled him with His *agape* love. (Acts 2:1-41)

Many Christians believe that the requirement to love as God loves begins with them rather than God! **Agape love begins and ends with God.** Man was never meant to mimic God's love or attempt to do the impossible. God's love is perfect love as in First

Corinthians chapter thirteen. We are meant to be vessels of His love for an outpouring to a lost world. God is jealous of His glory and will not share it with another. **God's plan is that a lost world sees His love flowing through His believers, which glorifies Him rather than the vessel of that *agape* love.**

What He does God require, but to let Him love others through releasing His *agape* love through His church. I often say to God, "If you want to love that person, then that's your problem and are you sure you know what you are doing? But I choose to allow the release of your *agape* love through me." Does this mean that I am to have no discernment? Of course not! As I yielded to the Holy Spirit and died to self, I've enjoyed the pleasure of seeing God's *agape* love flowing through me. I no longer want to be an impediment to His love, but to release His loving kindness to the world around me. He wants us to see the falleness of the world around us, well knowing the wrath of God against the wicked, and to pray that somehow the wicked might see the love of God through Christ's sacrifice on the cross and His forgiveness working through us. God's love is discerning and knows the hearts of men! God's love requires justice, which was achieved by Jesus on the cross for those who would be saved. It is the Holy Spirit of God that through grace saves men. Mercy is part of the gift of grace that means, in part, that men don't get what they deserve only because of the work of Christ on the cross purchased or redeemed man from the penalty of God's wrath and judgment!

> "For God so loved (agapao) the world, that he gave his only Son, that whoever believes in him should not perish but have eternal life." (John 3:16)

God's love is sacrificial in that he gave His only Son to die on the cross for the punishment that we deserved! His desire for justice was satisfied at His Son's expense.

God's wrath was appeased, atoned for, reconciled, or propitiated by the blood of Christ on the cross for those who are or will be His sheep. *"We have an advocate with the Father, Jesus Christ the righteous. He is the propitiation for our sins, and not for ours only but also for the sins of the whole world."* (1 John 2:1-2) This is what God's sacrificial agape love means. It cost God the pain of sacrificing His only Son for us. Saving or costly grace comes only from God. It is not a work of man. We are to be His instruments reflecting His grace and loving kindness to a fallen world.

The measure of our love for God is our priorities and obedience. Augustine, the fourth century Bishop of Hippo, explained that our sin is simply a reflection of our love priorities. I may have a choice on Sunday to go fishing or go to church. My choice reflects on what I love more, the fellowship of the brethren and worshiping God or my love of fishing. My sins in life were simply a reflection of bad choices I made because I didn't love God more than those bad choices. Therefore my sin is due to my failure to love God more than the lure of the world and its temptations. The more I love God the better choices I make and the less sin and temptation there is in my life. It is God's love in me that changes me from the inside out.

There is much confusion in the church about the understanding of personal sin. Sin is distinguished from transgression, which means breaking the Mosaic Law and iniquity, which means twistedness, deceptive, speaking half-truths, injustice, wickedness, and unrighteousness. Christ has shown us that sin, (*hamartia* the word used in Greek for sin means to miss the mark for an archer or wander from the path), is much more than breaking or transgressing one of the Ten Commandments. Sin is also about not loving and not making God first in our lives. The rich young ruler in Luke 18:18-23 claimed to obey the Mosaic Law completely but loved his money and position more than Jesus which is sin.

I was driving home one night from a very long hard day and I felt the nudge of the Spirit to stop and see a family in need on my way home. I didn't stop because I was hungry and tired. That was my excuse but I had sinned because my love of self and fulfilling of personal needs were greater than my love of God. I didn't break or transgress God's moral law but I disobeyed Him by prioritizing my love of self and fulfilling my personal needs as being greater than my love of and obedience to God. When we love God we make Him first. Obedience to Him becomes our first priority because we love Him. The more we love Him the more we will love others.

I looked back at *The Love Boat* and noted a staircase that went from the bottom deck to the top deck. The staircase was shaped like a triangle with people going up one way and then coming down the other. People were moving from the bottom deck to the top deck and back down to the lower levels. Those that got to the top deck could only stay there for a few moments, since they would fall down and cry convicted by their sin. They seemed to be changed and then went back to the lower decks to share what happened to them. Those that had gone up to the top deck with a sense of the futility of their ways and in need of God to shine his love through them were changed. There were also people that made it part way up to the upper deck and then placed their hands in front of their faces and hastily retreated. Some men chose to stay in the lower decks rather than come to meet the God of love on the top deck. These men were pleased with their own efforts to love their brother and saw no need to receive God's *agape* love!

It seems so ironic that it is only those with a broken and contrite spirit can see the futility of trying to love like God. Our confession is that men cannot fulfill the great commission of God to love their neighbor as themselves without the help of the Holy Spirit. Out of our inadequacy comes the adequacy of the Holy Spirit. God wants to pour his *agape* love into an empty vessel. The release of the spirit and flow of God's love requires the death of a man and his works. God will do through men what we cannot do for ourselves. My prayer was; **"Lord make me a vehicle for your sacrificial *agape* love. I understand that your love requires commitment, sacrifice, and obedience in me. Your *agape* love does not excuse lawlessness."**

There is an important body of Bible doctrine that underlies what Scripture teaches about *agape* love. Many people think divine love and sound theology are opposed to each other. Martyn Lloyd-Jones wrote about this very thing in his book, *The Love of God*:

> *"The great tendency in this present century has been to put up as antitheses the idea of God as a God of love on the one side, and theology or dogma or doctrine on the other. Now the average person has generally taken up such a position as follows: "You know, I am not interested in your doctrine. Surely the great mistake the church has made throughout the centuries is all this talk about dogma, all this doctrine of sin, and the doctrine of the Atonement, and this idea of justification and sanctification. Of course there are some people who may be interested in that kind of thing; they may enjoy reading and arguing about it, but as for myself," says this man, "there does not seem to be any truth in it; all I say is that God is love." So he puts up this idea of God as love over and against all these doctrines, which the church has taught throughout the centuries.5"*

This simplistic and unbalanced view of God's love is what I call **Sloppy Agape** or **that love which knows no boundaries and an oversimplification of the divine love of God and who God is! Balanced love knows God's justice and wrath as well as His love. Balanced love recognizes boundaries, which are articulated in church doctrines. It is that sloppy love that thinks God loves everybody and everything, including the wicked.** It is the modern attitude that "God loves everybody so why can't we just get along. You do your thing and I will do mine. God loves everyone no matter what they do!" This false concept of God's love promotes hedonism, social injustice, immorality, socialism, and communism. We may think that because God's love is unmerited and given

---

5   D. Martyn Lloyd-Jones, *The Love of God*, (Wheaton, IL: Crossway Books, 1994), 51.

freely by grace that it demands nothing from the recipient of that love in return. If God loves me no matter what I do and demands nothing in return, then this false concept undermines God's call for personal righteousness, obedience, and holiness! Instead, we are to love that which God loves but also to hate those who hate God and practice lawlessness. We are to hate sin! His love demands personal holiness, justice, obedience, and righteousness from the recipients of His love.

"They speak against you with malicious intent; your enemies take your name in vain! Do I not hate those who hate you, O Lord? And do I not loathe those who rise up against you? I hate them with complete hatred; I count them my enemies." (David speaking in Ps. 139:20-22.)

> *"For many deceivers have gone out into the world, those who do not confess the coming of Jesus Christ in the flesh. Such a one is the deceiver and the antichrist. Watch yourselves, so that you may not lose what we have worked for, but may win a full reward. Everyone who goes on ahead and does not abide in the teaching of Christ, does not have God. Whoever abides in the teaching has both the Father and the Son. If anyone comes to you and does not bring this teaching, do not receive him into your house or give him any greeting, for whoever greets him takes part in his wicked works."* (2nd John 7-11) Initially, it seems unloving not to be hospitable but in an effort to be "loving" many Christians actually encourage unregenerate people. Unmerited hospitality subtly implies approval of bad behavior and thus we *"take part in these wicked works."*

"If anyone has no love for the Lord, let him be accursed. Our Lord, come!" (1 Cor. 16:22) Jesus wept over Jerusalem but rebuked the Pharisees strongly in Matthew chapter 23. Some would say that

Jesus was unloving! To love someone is to warn and rebuke him. Is it unloving not to warn people that they are going to Hell unless they repent?

> *"The fear of the Lord is hatred of evil. Pride and arrogance and the way of evil and perverted speech I hate."* (Prov. 8:13)

We are to love our brother and respect and honor those in authority over us, but make no excuse for evil. *"Honor everyone. Love (agape) the brotherhood. Fear God. Honor the emperor."* (1 Pet. 2:17)

We cannot love what God hates! Remember, Peter is writing at a time when evil Nero was emperor and was soon to crucify him upside down. Peter instructs the church to honor authority, not love that authority, but give it the respect the office is due even when it is evil. We are to love the brotherhood or assembly of Christians and reach out in loving kindness and discernment to the world around us. God's love cost Him the sacrifice of His own Son for us. We in turn are called to sacrifice all and come follow Him because He first loved us and follow His example. **God's *agape* love is a free gift yet demands all from us!** It is like a man who sells all to buy a very expensive and most elegant diamond ring for his bride to be. The ring is given as a free love gift, but if she accepts it then she has to leave all, serve, obey, and cleave to her husband.

"If anyone would come after me, let him deny himself and take up his cross and follow me. For whoever would save his life will lose it, but whoever loses his life for my sake and the gospel's will save it. For what does it profit a man to gain the whole world and forfeit his soul? For what can a man give in return for his soul? For whoever is ashamed of me and of my words in this <u>adulterous and sinful generation, of him will the Son of Man also be ashamed when he comes in</u> the glory of his Father with the holy angels." (Mark 8:34-36)

*"This is my commandment, that you love one another as I have loved you. Greater love has no one than this, **<u>that someone lay down his life for his friends</u>**."* [Agape love requires personal sacrifice,

dying to self, and obedience] "**_You are my friends if you do what I command you_**. *No longer do I call you servants, for the servant does not know what his master is doing; but I have called you friends, for all that I have heard from my Father I have made known to you. You did not choose me, but I chose you and appointed you that you should go and bear fruit and that your fruit should abide, so that whatever you ask the Father in my name, he may give it to you. These things I command you, so that you will love one another.*" (John 15:12-17)

A return to an understanding of the biblical balance between God's love and his righteous wrath against sinners is desperately needed in today's church. It is beautifully expressed in Exodus 34:6-7. "*The Lord, the Lord, a God merciful and gracious, slow to anger, and abounding in steadfast love and faithfulness, **keeping steadfast love** for thousands, forgiving iniquity and transgression and sin, but who will **by no means clear the guilty**, visiting the iniquity of the fathers on the children and the children's children, to the third and the fourth generation.*"

God requires us to do what is impossible: to agape love others with the perfect unselfish agape love with which He agape loves us! This is impossible for man without the enabling power of the Holy Spirit! We are not called to agape love others in our own strength but to be a channel of the Holy Spirit and God's agape love to our brothers in Christ and a lost world. Agape love does not excuse lawlessness but in love confronts lawlessness.

Agape love produces justice and demands punishment for wickedness. This in turn is the foundation of civil government. It is because of God's wrath and the certain eternal damnation of the wicked that motivates us, through God's Agape love, to warn the wicked and to demand governments to pass laws encouraging moral values.

Chapter 9

POSTMODERNISM

I heard a scream from a man who was in obvious distress and very confused. He told me that he'd been thrown off the ship *"The Postmodern"* from the Tolerance Cruise Line located in Thyatira, Turkey. He was a young man probably in his early thirties who stated he had been looking for spiritual meaning in his life. He stated he joined a church called the Emergent Church and was drawn in by the contemporary music, casual clothes, and the lack of any judgmental attitudes or statements from the pulpit. They had chosen to do church differently. They taught there were neither absolutes nor certainty about theology, although they had a proper and humble confidence in God. They taught that words weren't absolute, only God was absolute.

To the Postmodern, truth is largely situational. They reject propositional truth. The reader might ask what is meant by propositional truth? A proposition is a logical statement or assertion that affirms that something is true or false. It assumes that truth is knowable. Christian theology or the study of God is based on a series of propositions such as "God cannot lie, God is Righteous, God is Holy, God is Good, God has created all things, God is one but three persons, God has revealed Himself through both general and special revelation, God hates evil and wickedness etc." These propositions boil down to expressing the basic elements of what God says about Himself in Scripture. Once basic foundational truths are rejected Christianity becomes untenable.

Christianity is not only about understanding certain propositional truths, such as Jesus died on the cross to atone for our sins, but about knowing Him personally or relationally.

Postmoderns teach that man is not capable of knowing truth unambiguously or with absolute certainty. This young man told us that he felt comfortable in the postmodern ship initially, in that it was a church that wasn't cluttered by any forms or rituals and there were no clear-cut objective definitions of sin or faith. The church seemed to be about discovering yourself rather than discovering God. The terms absolute truth, authority, infallibility, inerrancy, revelation, objective truths were pooh-poohed as being old fashioned, rigid, stone age, and anti-intellectual. They were neo-orthodox in that they presented a new way of thinking. It was Christianity-Lite or called "The Emergent Church" and easy to believe in that it didn't conflict with contemporary lifestyles.

Where did postmodern thinking start? It began in the Enlightenment with increasing skepticism about truth, particularly supernatural truth. The "I" became the measure of all things. Rene Descartes (1596-1650) and other enlightenment thinkers believed that human reason was the measure of all truth and arbiter of reality. Descartes and other enlightenment thinkers emphasized the human ability to find truth through reason alone. Immanuel Kant (1724-1804) denied any objective reality; there is only our experience. This line of thought makes man the measure of all things and emphasizes human autonomy.

These enlightenment thoughts were summarized in the American Thomas Paine's book, *The Age of Reason.* (1794) Paine was an American founding father who criticized institutional religion and the legitimacy of the Bible. He advocated reason to replace revelation in understanding God and man. He was a deist and loudly criticized for his critique of institutionalized religion and was eventually ostracized. At the time of his death only six people attended his funeral, yet his thoughts have been slowly incorporated into what is now called *Secular Humanism*, the majority religion in America today. Humanism rejects God, the Bible, the supernatural, and all religious dogma as a basis of morality and decision-making. Man is the center of life and meaning. He finds the meaning of right and wrong in himself and his secular culture. Truth is relative and is constantly changing along with current secular cultural and ethical values. Americans prefer the title secular humanism rather than more primitive terms like polytheistic paganism or Gnostic deism, which is really what humanism, is all about.

Today in America, there has been a rejection of historical Christianity and its basic tenants of *sola gratia* (only grace), *sola fide* (only faith), *solo Christo* (only Christ), *sola scriptura* (only Scripture), and *soli Deo Gloria* (to God alone be glory). There is no longer a need for the Bible since man can find truth through personal experience and reason! The truth of Scripture has been displaced by the internal emotions and feelings. External truth is measured by "what is your spirit telling you?"

Secular Humanism rejects the Bible and the supernatural and espouses a humanistic form of ethics, law, justice, and decision-making based on reason, evidence, and the scientific method. John Dewey authored the *Humanistic Manifesto* in 1933. He argued for no creator, no creation, and no moral absolutes! I am sure Thomas Paine would be delighted to see America today, since it has largely accepted and confirmed his beliefs.

The church fathers began with Scripture as the Word of God and reasoned from it. They built their theology on what God said in Scripture. Modern man begins with himself and builds his theology from experience and observation of the culture around him and uses his life experience to interpret Scripture and build his understanding of God.

Modern theology is based on a pluralistic narcissism and rejects classical foundational Christianity as expressed in the great creeds (Apostle's creed, Nicene and Athanasiun creeds) and confessions of the reformation such as the Belgic Confession of 1561, Heidelberg Catechism of 1563, and the later Westminster confession of 1646 and the Baptist confession of 1689. The creeds and confessions of the church are not meant to be considered equal with Scripture but declarative and interpretative of what Scripture clearly states as truth. The word creed derives from the Latin *Credo*, I believe. Creeds are especially important today since most Christians don't know what they believe! Their spirituality is based on their spiritual experience rather than good solid doctrine. Much of the truth in these old creeds was put into the old classic hymns, which are rarely sung, in contemporary church services.

Athanasius, who lived 296-373 AD, was a great defender of the faith. The Athanasian Creed states: "Whosoever will be saved: before all things it is necessary that he hold the catholic faith." The word catholic with a small "c" means universal or the generally accepted norm for that time (Fourth Century). *This assumes certain knowable, unchangeable, objective truths as revealed in the Word of God. These truths are eternal truths that are the same yesterday, today and forever.* (Heb. 13:8) If truth could change with time it could not be truth. We trust scientific truth, such as certain laws of the physical sciences, to explain our world and the universe around us because these laws are eternal truth. We have assumed that these physical laws are eternal; yet we doubt that the eternal truths of God are immutable, eternal, and also unchanging!

Paul in 2 Timothy 1:13 warns Timothy as follows: *Follow the pattern of the sound words that you have heard from me in the faith and love that are in Christ Jesus.* Later, Paul warns Timothy in chapter 4:3-4: *For the time is coming when people will not endure sound teaching, but having itching ears they will accumulate for themselves teachers to suit their passions and will turn away from listening to the truth and wander into myths.* Paul was warning about being culturally relevant in the first century!

There are certain immovable boundaries in Christianity and some theologians are trying to move the goal posts. Once these are removed this is no longer Christianity. The ancient paths are where we will find peace.

> *"Stand by the roads, and look, and ask for the*
> *ancient paths, where the good way is; and walk in*

*it and find rest for your souls. But they said, 'We
will not walk in it.'* (Jer. 6:16)

Balanced Christianity avoids barren intellectualism and dead orthodoxy without over emphasis on spiritual experiences at the expense of doctrine and foundational eternal truths. Experience based Christianity, without a biblical foundation, is shallow and superficial and produces a vulnerability to deception that is exploited by the postmoderns and the cults.

The postmoderns emphasize tolerance. This is expressed in an outright refusal to say that anyone else is wrong. They don't believe that the Bible can be taken literally nor define absolute behavior. Church members expressed a love of philosophy, leftist politics, and situational ethics. When there is no absolute truth, everyone can be right! Sin was defined as hurting somebody else, rather than breaking God's law. You were free to act out any of your sexual urges as long as you didn't hurt anybody. Truth evolves, according to their teaching, so that current societal mores play a large role in defining what is right and wrong. They used the example of their understanding of homosexuality and whether or not this is a sin. The biblical statements on homosexuality were considered old-fashioned, narrow-minded, and judgmental.

After all, wasn't truth evolving? There wasn't one central truth but many truths! Tolerance meant that we tolerate anything but that the Bible is absolute truth! Tolerance means, do not judge, or more subtly, do not think critically. There was more fear of being intolerant than fearing and displeasing God. Their emphasis was on right living rather than right belief. They felt that true faith in Jesus was not a matter of creedal orthodoxy but in doing the right thing. Many of the leaders were Universalists meaning that you don't have to convert to any particular religion to find God as long as you're a good person and you do right things, you'll be accepted by God.

Since Christ "came to fulfill the law," they felt they were no longer under the Ten Commandments or old covenant but the New Covenant. The New Covenant was to love your brother and God.

They were under grace and not the law! They widely believed the error and heresy of Marcion (85-160 AD).

Marcion was an ancient Gnostic heretic condemned by the church for teaching that Jesus abolished the Old Testament law by establishing His New Covenant, and therefore the Old Testament could be removed in its entirety from the Canon of Scripture as well as certain New Testament epistles. These teachers spoke of the "God of the Old Testament as angry and vengeful as opposed to the God of the New Testament, the God of Love!" They seem to forget that Jesus quoted extensively from the Old Testament, and he said he came to establish the law. The foundation of the early church was the Old Testament and the centrality of God's perfect law. To imply that there were two different Gods in the Bible, one angry and unloving, and another loving and forgiving, reflects ancient occult beliefs of dualism, Gnosticism, and Manichaeism. It is absolutely unbiblical but postmodern teachers seem to get away with it.

The reader may be unfamiliar with Gnosticism, but a basic understanding of this pagan teaching will equip the reader to understand the church of the twenty-first century. The word *gnosis* is the Greek word for knowledge. It stems from ancient Greek concern on how the world and creation came into being. How could a good God allow for the existence of evil? If God is a Holy God then He could not create evil. God somehow limited Himself in creation. Evil, they reasoned, was from the material universe and therefore, the material world must be evil. This means we have a dualistic universe of good and evil not unlike the ancient dualism, (*ying yang*), of Chinese Daoism. Once God has been removed from the stigma of creating a fallen world, then man becomes the center of the material world.

Man looks for the "God within." Gnostic leaders were very elitist and like the emerging church leaders culturally sophisticated and narcissistic with man's pursuit of "The God Within Man" being the center. With man as the center, the Gnostic becomes very syncretistic and incorporates a variety of Christian, Jewish, Platonic, occult, and Eastern religious theological thought. They believe in what is called Doceticism, which comes from the Greek word *dokein to seem or to appear*. Jesus was said to only have seemed to die on the cross but in actuality it was an illusion and a good God saved His son from death by substituting another man who *appeared* to be Jesus dying on the cross. Many of the Gnostics were banished by the early church to Medina and Mecca in Arabia where they influenced Mohammad. This same Gnostic belief about the substitution of another in the cross for Christ was repeated after 622 AD in the Koran. To the Gnostics and Muslims alike, the very idea of a Good God allowing His Son to die on the cross was morally and intellectually repugnant. They fail to understand that if Jesus didn't die on the cross, then there would be no sacrificial death or atonement for sin. If there was no resurrection, then there would be no proof that Jesus was indeed the son of God. If no resurrection then no hope of heaven, or any Christianity. Paul tells us in First Corinthians 15:13-14:

> *"Now if Christ is proclaimed as raised from the dead, how can some of you say that there is no resurrection of the dead? But if there is no resurrection of the dead, then not even Christ has been raised. And if Christ has not been raised, then our preaching is in vain and your faith is in vain."*

The apostle John warns the church about those who deny the actual physical death in the flesh of Jesus on the cross for our sins as the spirit of the antichrist! *"Beloved do not believe every spirit but test the spirits to see whether they are from God, for many false prophets have gone out into the world. By this you know the Spirit of God: every spirit that confesses that Jesus Christ has come in the flesh is from God, and every spirit that does not confess Jesus is not from God. This is the spirit of the antichrist."* (1 John 4:1-3) The thought that Jesus' death on the cross was some type of apparition or false vision is from the pit of Hell and the very new age spirit of the antichrist.

103

The idea that Gnostics had secret knowledge is thought by some to be traced back in part to Simon Magnus, the magician in Acts chapter eight. Simon offered money to purchase the power of the Holy Spirit. Church tradition suggests that Simon became an early leader of the Gnostics, and the term *Simony* means the merchandising of the things of God. The spirit of Simon seems to be very much alive in the church today. Gnosticism rejects rational knowledge. They believe that the five senses, such as touch, taste, sight, sound, and smell could be trusted as a measure of truth. They rejected rational investigation and replaced it with mysticism. The Gnostic god was unknowable and impersonal. Man became the center and found the "god within himself" just like Satan said in the Garden of Eden, *you will become like God, knowing good and evil* (Gen. 3:5). Gnosticism is about the struggle for truth within man versus that truth which is outside, His church and Scripture.

It focused on a "spiritual feeling" type of knowledge that was not checked by the Word of God. "The spirit told me such and such." This is a dangerous type of unbridled subjectivism. It is a feeling type of faith that is not biblical. The goal is to bypass the rational mind, which cannot be trusted, and to achieve spiritual enlightenment or *gnosis*. To the Gnostic the cause of suffering, wars, and rebellion in this world is not sin but ignorance. Salvation is found in mystical enlightenment or an altered consciousness through self-knowledge.

This type of faith that says, "it is just me and God" is very American and individualistic. The self becomes the source of authentication of the revelation of God rather than Scripture, church creeds, and church fellowship. This is where many Christians are today. Peter told us that *no prophesy of Scripture is of any private interpretation* (2 Pet. 1:20). We are to never take God's Word out of the context of the totality of all Scripture. All mystical feelings are to be checked by ALL of Scripture. Individual Scriptures are often used to justify unbiblical behavior. This was done by Satan, who took Scriptures out of context, (Ps. 91:11-12) during the temptation of Jesus, in Matthew and Luke chapters four.

> *"Then the devil took him to the holy city and set him on the pinnacle of the temple and said to him, "If you are the Son of God, throw yourself down, for it is written, " 'He will command his angels concerning you,' and " 'On their hands they will bear you up, lest you strike your foot against a stone.' "* Quoted from (Ps. 91:11-12; Matt, 4:5-6)

Satan knows Scripture better than any living human and often uses it deftly to bring confusion to the church. We must always seek the whole council of God through the entirety of Scripture, prayer, bible commentary of great men of God, and the council of godly fellow Christians.

Paul preached directly to the Gnostics and the Greek philosophers in First Corinthians chapter one. It is not the wisdom of this world that saves us, but the most unintellectual thought and seemingly foolish concept to many. *"Jesus Christ and Him crucified!"* (1 Cor. 2:2)

"Where is the one who is wise? Where is the scribe? Where is the debater of this age? Has not God made foolish the wisdom of the world? For since, in the wisdom of God, the world did not know God through wisdom, it pleased God through the folly of what we preach to save those who believe. For Jews demand signs and Greeks seek wisdom, but we preach Christ crucified, a stumbling block to Jews and folly to Gentiles, but to those who are called, both Jews and Greeks, Christ the power of God and the wisdom of God. For the foolishness of God is wiser than men, and the weakness of God is stronger than men." (1 Cor. 1:20-25)

In summary, postmodernism is a pluralistic religious relativism, which emphasizes tolerance rather than absolute truth. Tolerance has replaced truth. **Their logic is oxymoron, or makes no logical sense, since it claims that the only absolute truth is that there is no absolute truth!** Different religions are considered largely cultural with competing truth claims; all of which have their cultural validity, but there is no single absolute truth or way to the true

105

God. This is religious multiculturalism. Jesus offends the postmodern by His exclusivity. This is best exemplified in John 14:6 where Jesus says, *"I am the way, the truth and the life and no one comes to the Father but by me!"* This can be expanded to say absolutely that Jesus is the only way, the only truth, the only way to real life, and the only way to the Father. How radical!

Ecumenism, or the principle of promoting unity among Christian churches and other faiths, makes attempts for unity but often at the expense of foundational Christian truth. Claims that "we all worship the same God, so why can't we get along," are often from the enemy of truth and lead to a compromised Gospel in the name of unity and brotherly love. We don't worship the same God as other religions, such as Islam, and there is no other God in Heaven or earth but Christ Jesus and His foundational truth is not negotiable!

Chapter 10

THE EMERGENT CHURCH

How do we reach the lost in a multicultural world? How do we present the gospel in the context of various cultures, ethnicity, age, race, language, and subcultures? This question has caused debate since the beginning of the missionary movement. The word used today is contextualization or in older terms accommodation, indigenization, and adaptation. These big words mean to communicate the gospel in meaningful terms to people of different cultures. In the American church, efforts have been made to reach out to the unchurched pagan world. These efforts are laudable but unfortunately have often resulted in a compromised gospel. In an effort to be relevant there is the danger of compromise and syncretism. The fear of many theologians is much rigidity may make the message irrelevant.

Contextualizing means to some theologians that because people and culture evolve, then theology or our understanding of Scriptures must also evolve with it! When the culture defines the understanding of Scripture, we have opened the door not only to heresy and apostasy, but also to the doctrines of demons! ***Truth never changes, if it did it wouldn't be truth***! We forget how radical the message of Christ was in his own time. It was so radical that religious men wanted to kill Him. The message of the gospel has never changed and remains as radical and anti-cultural today as it was in biblical times. The message of *come and die, give up all and follow me,* can never be made inoffensive.

In Latin America contextualization resulted in "Liberation Theology". In the American church movements have resulted in a new "Generous Orthodoxy." Many in the Emergent church movement have adopted the philosophy that cultural relevance means incorporating cultural moral values, and religious beliefs into the gospel message and church life. This is syncretism, Christian pluralism, or mixture, which has brought much confusion. Once the camel's nose is under the tent all is lost and Christianity is no longer unique or radical. Postmodernism is a theology of neutrality that no longer confronts the culture but has joined it!

Many Christians have been so marginalized by the current pagan culture, that orthodox Christianity is an embarrassment. Many church leaders "tone down" the hard truths of scripture such as teachings on marriage, divorce, homosexuality, eternal damnation, and abortion. In an attempt to make Christianity relevant to the culture, they have made it irrelevant!

Scripture reminds us that Jesus said, *"If you abide in my word, you are truly my disciples and you will know the truth, and the truth will set you free,"* (John 8:31-32). Postmodern man believes he can find truth apart from abiding in God. These men, who are searching for truth, will not find it apart from Jesus Christ and scripture.

The mystery of the redeeming work of Christ is only understood by those that are saved. Unregenerate man makes his own form of pseudo-Christianity where man is the center, and the cross is repugnant to his flesh. The cross offends and is a stumbling block to false religions. Man doesn't need the work of the cross since he thinks he can save himself. This is the foolishness of man. This new form of spirituality or pseudo-Christianity is nothing new but a mixture of Gnosticism, humanism, paganism, postmodernism, and deism.

From an early start Gnosticism has plagued the church in many different colors. Today there is interest in extra-biblical Gnostic literature such as *The Gospel of Thomas, the Apocalypse of Peter, The Gospel of Philip,* and *The Apocryphon of John.*

Transcendentalists such as Ralph Waldo Emerson, Walt Whitman, Herman Melville, William James, Henry David Thoreau, Mary Baker Eddy, and other Boston intellectuals emerged in the nineteenth century America with a Gnostic message followed by theologians like Hegel, Bultman, Niebuhr, Tillich, C. G. Jung, Harry Emerson Fosdick, Norman Vincent Peale and the "Human Potential Movement" in the twentieth century. This has resulted in a church that pursues personal happiness and the finding of meaning of the self above all! Doctrine, church traditions, and the sacraments are dumbed down or ignored in pursuit of inclusiveness. The church has become self-authenticating, rather than Scripture, ancient church confessions, traditions, and creedal statements. America is now proudly called a "Post Christian" Nation!! Many of the mainline churches in America are also "Post Christian" since they no longer hold Christian core values and doctrines. They are Christian in name only!

Recently in 2009, U.S. President Barack Obama said in Turkey: "We do not consider ourselves a Christian nation or a Jewish nation or a Muslim nation. We consider ourselves a nation of citizens who are bound by ideals and a set of values." Obama was soundly trounced by Christian pundits for making that statement, but in actuality he was correct. America considers herself a Christian nation, but is not. Our religion is a type of pagan deistic humanism.

Special extra-biblical revelation, progressive levels of revelation, and their own extra-biblical Scriptures characterize Gnosticism. Rigid asceticism was often taught to combat the desires of the flesh. Often, they claimed Angelic visitations with special revelation. Many of the cults are basically Gnostic in origin such as Scientology, Mormonism, Jehovah's Witness, Christian Science, Masonry, and many others. The poison of the Gnostics is very much with us today.

Many believe that man was born innocent and good, as did the heretic Pelagius in the fourth century. He was influenced by Celtic and Druidic pagan philosophy, which has always subverted Christian truth. If man is born good, then he is capable of making right decisions without the mediating grace of God. Man becomes as God finding right or wrong in himself. Sin becomes a mere breach of etiquette and a self-defeating behavior. This pagan narcissistic philosophy of the goodness of man was rejected by Augustine and later church councils. The Chart Book is clear. Man is born in sin, not innocence, and can never ever choose what is good or choose God without the regenerational help of the Holy Spirit. (Eph. 2:8-9) God's assessment of man is clearly expressed in Psalm 14:1-3.

> *"The fool says in his heart, "There is no God." They are corrupt, they do abominable deeds, there is none who does good. The Lord looks down from heaven on the children of man, to see if there are any who understand, who seek after God. They have all turned aside; together they have become corrupt; there is none who does good, not even one."*

Men seek the wisdom of pagans, which is the "Universal Mystery" that we are all divine like God. The creator becomes Sophia or mother earth! Sexual roles become reversed, and God becomes bisexual, both mother and father! Mankind's sexual roles become confused, and this results in the acceptance of homosexuality as normative. The attention is shifted from the Creator God above to Mother Earth below. This has resulted in pagan environmentalism, climate change emphasis, and other efforts to "save the earth." The United Nations sees its major function as the "Loving Care of the Earth." They plan to bring all nations together for the "Great Work" of saving the earth by appealing to occultic ecologic spirituality. This new spirituality is called "Progressive Spirituality," "Integrated Spirituality," or "Spirituality with Global Consciousness."

To accomplish this goal there must be a merging of Eastern religious spirituality, Muslim, Jewish, neopaganism, animism, shamanism, Gnosticism, with Christian beliefs. Under the name of "social justice" and the cry to "save the earth" they plan to institute one world government. The essence of the new world religion is a religious experience rather than doctrine making us all one. This requires syncretism or a merging of different religions into one, which is exactly what is happening through the postmodern emergent church and the ecumenical movement whose motto, is "Why can't we all get along?" This question is a guilt trip to make Christians feel guilty for disagreeing with people of different faiths. The postmodern regard the Bible as a "living document" open to interpretation according to societal values. Biblical truth never changes! We must not forget that Christianity is very exclusive, and our doctrines are non-negotiable. This means that true Christianity will likely be progressively marginalized in this post Christian pantheistic modern world.

> *"I am astonished that you are so quickly deserting him who called you in the grace of Christ and are turning to a different gospel not that there is another one, but there are some who trouble you and want to distort the gospel of Christ. But even if we or an angel from heaven should preach to you a gospel contrary to the one, we preached to you, let him be accursed. As we have said before, so now I say again: If anyone is preaching to you a gospel contrary to the one you received, let him be accursed."* (Gal. 1:6-9)

Modern man rejects God's assessment of himself as a hopeless sinner without any hope of reformation without Christ. He sees himself as a good person but acknowledges some minor failures. The central goal of his life is to be happy and feel good about himself. This means no guilt. Guilt is assuaged by the affirmation of other sinners and a gospel where sin is no longer preached or even mentioned. Modern man's problems are thought to be the result of variety of environmental/cultural/genetic and situational factors. Biblical sins such as murder, rape, adultery, theft, and many others are now labeled addictions such as alcoholism, drug addiction, sex addiction, or psychosocial adjustment problems. Man is no longer responsible for his actions because his actions are due to environmental/genetic factors beyond his control.

This is out right cultural/environmental/psychological/biological determinism. Determinism is the philosophical view that every event, including human behavior, and action, is causally determined by prior events. It means that there is a predetermined unbroken chain of prior occurrences that cause man's actions. This makes the free will to make moral choices impossible and if the free will to make moral choices is impossible, then man is no longer responsible for his actions. Man is no longer a free agent able to choose between right and wrong. Therefore, man is a victim of prior circumstances such as bad parenting. He no longer has guilt because he is just a victim of extraneous factors that he couldn't control. Determinists have no answer for variation or error.

A child may be born in a good family and have all the privileges that modern society brings yet turn out badly. Similarly, another child may be brought up in a horrible, dysfunctional family situation with limited opportunity for an education or other opportunities yet turn out to be a model leader and citizen. Philosophical determinanism or fatalism can provide no answers for variation and error and therefore it is a bankrupt pseudophilosophical theory without substance used by the postmodernists to explain away sin.

Astrology is a form of spiritual determinism and a pseudoscience dealing with the supposed influence of the heavenly bodies on human character and destiny. The desire to understand the future and influence its events has shown itself in all lands and ages particularly ancient Babylon. But knowledge of the future does not lie within the scope of man's natural powers; "divination" therefore has always been an attempt to gain the help of beings possessing knowledge and power transcending those of man like fortune tellers, astrologers, palm readers, and other forms of divination (i.e. the demonic). The Lord speaks through Isaiah and rebukes Babylon in chapter 47 of the Book of Isaiah.

> *"You are wearied with your many counsels; let them stand forth and save you, those who divide the heavens, who gaze at the stars, who at the new moons make known. What shall come upon you."* (Isa. 47:13)

Hindu concepts of *Karma* and reincarnation are other examples of spiritual determinism and fatalism which brings nothing more than bondage and enslavement by telling men that their low cast status is essentially their own fault due to sin in a previous life. This benefits the upper classes that desire to keep men in servitude.

The problem with determinism is that it removes hope of self-reformation from man. If my life and actions are determined by factors beyond my control, why should I try to change since there is nothing I can do about it? It's in the stars or it's my karma. A deterministic view of man only produces despair and hopelessness. If I can never overcome the power of social/environmental/psychological/biological/genetic/spiritual factors that have shaped my personality and behavior, then I am like the French existentialist Albert Camus who concluded that life had no meaning!

Postmoderns use determinism to explain man's actions yet ironically believe that man can partly overcome these genetic/environmental/cultural problems with proper training, education, and encouragement to make good choices. They believe man is born good and without sin and therefore potentially correctable and reformable! They fail to see the inherent logical conflict between determinism and the ability to change man.

American jurisprudence increasingly minimizes sin by giving light sentences for horrible crimes. This undermines the role of Government to protect citizens and punish wickedness. The Roman General Scipio was quoted by Augustine to have said: "What harmony is to music; justice is to society. A society that lacks justice cannot survive."

The deterministic understanding of sin in America has transformed the penal/jurisprudence system to a system that has switched from biblical punishment to efforts of restitution of man using psychosocial methods. This is no longer called punishment, but rehabilitation. The Bible is very clear. Man is born a sinner, cannot be rehabilitated, and is without hope without Christ as his Lord!

> *"The heart is deceitful above all things, and desperately sick; who can understand it?"* (Jer. 17:9)

As Christians we understand that man's heart is sick and beyond help. The only cure for this sick helpless man with a sick heart is a complete cardiac transplant. Those who have a saving faith in Jesus will be given a new heart. It is this new heart that allows true repentance followed by changed behavior. Yes, in unredeemed man, you can with various incentives produce superficial outward changes in behavior, but never a changed heart. This can never happen without the redemptive work of Christ to produce a spiritually transformed heart.

The Bible speaks of the transformation of man or metamorphosis of sinner to saint. This is akin to the change from a pupa to a butterfly.

> *"Do not be conformed to this world but be <u>transformed</u> (μεταμορφόω or metamorphoo) by the renewal of your mind, that by testing you may discern what is the will of God, what is good and acceptable and perfect."* (Rom. 12.2) *"And we all, with unveiled face, beholding the glory of the Lord, are being <u>transformed</u> into the same image from one degree of glory to another. For this comes from the Lord who is the Spirit."* (2nd Corinthians 3:18)

Man, like the pupa or worm, is not to be conformed (changed behavior) but be transformed (changed into a different form or transfigured into the likeness of Christ or like a beautiful butterfly).

> *"And you were dead in the trespasses and sins in which you once walked, following the course of this world, following the prince of the power of the air, the spirit that is now at work in the sons of disobedience—among whom we all once lived in the passions of our flesh, carrying out the desires of the body and the mind, and were by nature children of wrath, like the rest of mankind. But God, being rich in mercy, because of the great love with which he loved us, even when we were dead in our trespasses, made us alive together with Christ—by grace you have been saved."*
> (Eph. 2:1-5)

All men are dead in trespasses and sins and follow worldly passions and values. All men are without hope and cannot be changed or transformed by worldly methods, unless the Holy Spirit converts them. Christ has made us alive by grace to be transformed into new creatures through Christ, Hallelujah!

Postmoderns believe that civilization is improving, and that man is the solution to the world's problems. Evolution was thought to be the proof of an evolving universe that is becoming increasingly perfected. After all, hasn't man gone to the moon! Isn't life better now with modern conveniences, indoor plumbing, rapid transportation, vaccines, modern medicine, antibiotics, etc.? Surely, no one would want to go back in time!

I thought, if postmodern man is so good and the world is doing so well, then I didn't see any reason why humanistic man thinks he needs God's help!

The postmodern leaders felt that past statements of faith were about drawing borders or boundaries, and this was a no-no since basically they did not accept absolute truth. Boundaries are thought of as rigid inflexible rules reflecting ancient cultural beliefs not relevant to modern man. If there is no absolute truth, or if truth is evolving, then there can never be any absolute boundaries on human behavior. Ethics have now become situational, which means any evil behavior such as murder, incest, or rape can be justified in the right situation. This is called antinomianism or against the law. Lawlessness leads to rebellion, anarchy, mob rule as well as hopelessness. Deep in his heart this distressed man knew this teaching was wrong and it brought him much confusion, depression, and a sense of hopelessness. He began to understand that neo-orthodoxy without strictly doctrinal content becomes meaningless.

I explained that no one could have knowledge of God without a set of propositions of truth and behavior. Without certain propositional truths, God becomes meaningless. To love God is to obey Him. To obey him is to know Him. Jesus states, *"I am the way, the truth, and the life; no one comes to the Father but through me!"* (John 14:4-5) He is the creator of all things, and the Bible is His Word. Jesus comes to rule and reign, to establish His Kingdom and Lordship.

There can be no compromise; ethics and truth are absolute! Jesus offends the postmodern mind with his claims of absolute truth and the requirement of submission to His Lordship and His rules of behavior. He is very intolerant, which the postmoderns hate! The certain reality of everlasting punishment and everlasting reward, as well as the resurrection of all men to judgment, is too much for the liberal postmodern mind. God has had to be reinvented to accommodate the liberal worldview. Now, God is like a Gnostic illusion with no meaning and distant from the affairs of men. Christianity stripped of its doctrinal content is no Christianity at all!

Peter in his second letter warns of false teaching and teachers and its consequences:

"These are waterless springs and mists driven by a storm. For them the gloom of utter darkness has been reserved. For, speaking loud boasts of folly, they entice by sensual passions of the flesh those who are barely escaping from those who live in error. They promise them freedom, but they themselves are slaves of corruption. For whatever overcomes a person, to that he is enslaved. For if, after they have escaped the defilements of the world through the knowledge of our Lord and Savior Jesus Christ, they are again entangled in them and overcome, the last state has become worse for them than the first.

For it would have been better for them never to have known the way of righteousness than after knowing it to turn back from the holy commandment delivered to them. What the true proverb says has happened to them: "The dog returns to its own vomit, and the sow, after washing herself, returns to wallow in the mire," (2 Pet. 2:17-22). The young man told me he was also taught that orthodoxy means right belief and orthopraxy means right living. He was taught that right living or orthopraxy then flows into right beliefs. This is just the opposite of what the church teaches. The church teaches that right belief or the essential doctrines of the church and study of his Word produce right behavior. To the leaders of this Emergent Church, the very nature of theology was one of conversation and dialogue rather than setting boundaries by accepting biblical law and definition of sin in Scripture.

This young man said all he wanted was happiness. After all doesn't every man have the right to life, liberty, property, prosperity, and happiness? These modern postmodern gurus promised all and most of all happiness. Happiness was left undefined, and every man was to define it for himself, but peace, pleasure, and prosperity were implied. To modern man the right to the pursuit of happiness is the end for which all men exist. How unfortunate and tragic because God does not promise happiness but promises something much better, JOY and PEACE. Happiness is from the word happenstance meaning it is situational. Joy is not situational but available to all who willingly serve our Lord, Jesus Christ. Joy is not contingent on our situation; rich or poor, sickness or health, but in all things, we are to rejoice. (I Thessalonians 5:16-18) The peace of Christ is different from the world's peace. (John 14:27) *"Peace I leave with you; my peace I give to you. Not as the world gives do I give to you. Let not your hearts be troubled, neither let them be afraid."*

The Puritan divines in 1648 summarized the collective wisdom of the ages in the Westminster Confession Question One. *"What is the chief end of man? Man' s chief end is **to glorify** God, (1 Cor. 10:31, Rom. 11:36) and **to enjoy** him for ever. (Ps. 73:25–28)"* and Question Two: *"What rule hath God given to direct us how we may* *glorify and enjoy him? The Word of God, which is contained in the Scriptures of the Old and New Testaments, (2 Tim. 3:16, Eph. 2:20) is the only rule to direct us how we may glorify and enjoy him. (1 John 1:3–4)"*

Suffering is the great enemy of the postmodern man and is to be avoided at all costs. The call of Christ is to suffer for Him and with Him is ignored and carefully avoided so not to offend.

"If the world hates you, know that it has hated me before it hated you. If you were of the world, the world would love you as its own; but because you are not of the world, but I chose you out of the world, therefore the world hates you. Remember the word that I said to you: 'A servant is not greater than his master.' If they persecuted me, they will also persecute you." (John 15:18-20)

Suffering is the cost of true discipleship and the reason many reject biblical Christianity. To promote a gospel that does not require the rejection of men and family and personal suffering is to promote a false gospel as in Mark 13:10-13: *"And the gospel must first be proclaimed to all nations. And when they bring you to trial and deliver you over, do not be anxious beforehand what you are to say, but say whatever is given you in that hour, for it is not you who speak, but the Holy Spirit. And brother will deliver brother over to death, and the father his child, and children will rise against parents and have them put to death. And you will be hated by all for my name's sake. But the one who endures to the end will be saved."*

This young man came under the conviction of the Holy Spirit and repented. He asked God for forgiveness, continual repentance, and His Lordship. We welcomed him home. I asked him why he was thrown off the ship. He told me that he asked too many questions and challenged the leadership humbly. So much for liberal tolerance!

Chapter 11

FALSE PROPHETS

I saw another ship covered in white paint with beautiful gold accents. This was another ship from the Prosperity Cruise Line, and it was called *True or False, Pay Your Money and Make Your Choice* from Pergamun, Turkey. This "Prophetic ship" had three levels. The bottom level was enclosed and the people within were chained to large oars that protruded from the hull of the ship. The upper decks were open and without railings. There were men walking about with long sticks with baskets attached to the end of the sticks. They were asking people for gold and money and even asked people who were swimming in the sea to contribute for a prophetic word in exchange for money. They threw nets overboard to catch men floating in the sea and draw them into their prosperity ship.

There appeared to be a type of store at the stern of the boat where people were selling books and tapes and there were little booths, which were for meeting with the prophet for personal prophecy, for a fee of course! The top level of the boat was the level of false prophets and was called "*The Way of Balaam*." (2 Pet. 2:15) They told people what they wanted to hear and proclaimed peace and prosperity for money.

> "Bold and willful, they do not tremble as they blaspheme the glorious ones, whereas angels,

*though greater in might and power, do not pro-
nounce a blasphemous judgment against them
before the Lord. But these, like irrational animals, creatures of instinct, born to be caught and
destroyed, blaspheming about matters of which
they are ignorant, will also be destroyed in their
destruction, suffering wrong as the wage for their
wrongdoing. They count it pleasure to revel in the
daytime. They are blots and blemishes, reveling in
their deceptions, while they feast with you. They
have eyes full of adultery, insatiable for sin. They
entice unsteady souls. They have hearts trained in
greed. Accursed children! Forsaking the right way,
they have gone astray. They have followed the
way of Balaam, the son of Beor, who loved gain
from wrongdoing, but was rebuked for his own
transgression; a speechless donkey spoke with
human voice and restrained the prophet's mad-
ness. These are waterless springs and mists driven
by a storm. For them the gloom of utter darkness
has been reserved. For, speaking loud boasts of
folly, they entice by sensual passions of the flesh
those who are barely escaping from those who
live in error. They promise them freedom, but they
themselves are slaves of corruption. For whatever
overcomes a person, to that he is enslaved."* (2
Pet. 2:10-19)

**They claimed to be Apostles. The prophecies had just
enough truth in them to make them believable to those without
much discernment. I remembered Paul's words in 2 Corinthians
11:13-15:**

*"For such men are false apostles, deceitful work-
men, disguising themselves as apostles of Christ.
And no wonder, for even Satan disguises himself*

as an angel of light. So it is no surprise if his servants, also, disguise themselves as servants of righteousness. Their end will correspond to their deeds."

The second level of the ship was called *"Mixture."* There were prophets at this level also telling people often just what they wanted to hear. There was mixture with some words coming from Scripture and some from God, and many words were given by divination.

The third level was the level of the *"True Prophets of God."* These men were kept in chains, and chained to the oars. They prophesied death and destruction to the wicked and to the false prophets. They called for true repentance. They mourned and wept for the condition of the church. They were called *"to root out, pull down, to destroy, and to throw down and then build and plant"* according to the word of Jeremiah 1:10. They were rejected as being harsh and unloving. People wondered how a loving God could speak such harsh words to his church. People wondered why they spoke warnings of calamity and great storms. Could this possibly be from God? There were some men from the second level who would go down and listen to the prophets speak and then go back up to the second level and repeat those words with their voice. They were stealing the words of the true prophets and using them as their own.

> *"Is not my word like fire, declares the Lord, and like a hammer that breaks the rock in pieces? Therefore, behold, I am against the prophets, declares the Lord, who steal my words from one another."* (Jer. 23:29)

I wondered, what is the measure of a true prophet of God? **The fruit of a true prophetic word must be to turn men away from their sin** according to Jeremiah 23:21-22:

> *"I did not send the prophets, yet they ran; I did
> not speak to them, yet they prophesied. But if
> they had stood in my council, then they would
> have proclaimed my words to my people, and
> <u>they would have turned them from their evil way,</u>
> and from the evil of their deeds."*

Many "prophetic ministries" validate their ministries with various "signs and wonders" such as filling teeth with gold, sprinkling people with gold dust, feathers, and various gem stones. People may fall "under the spirit" or bark like dogs, roar like lions, or develop uncontrollable laughing. Female angels may heal people and a variety of other mystical happenings may occur in their meetings. None of these "spiritual manifestations" are recorded in the Bible, which makes them very suspect! Some critics dismiss these out of hand as bogus. Both charismatics and non-charismatics fail to realize that these weird mystical manifestations are indeed very spiritual and real, but often from the wrong spiritual source: the demonic. When men have unbridled ambition, they become vulnerable to any force that gives them power and adulation. They attract camp followers who are spiritual voyeurs entertained and excited by any demonstration of the supernatural. This search for the supernatural can easily lead into spiritual deception and Satan is very happy to accommodate these vulnerable ambitious "Christians" with all types of signs and wonders.

Miracles attract the skeptical as well as the believers. In biblical times many thousands and possibly as many as one million came to see Jesus, but only 120 waited for Him in the upper room! Herod mocked God but enjoyed the spectacle of the miracle worker or a good magic show.

> *"When Herod saw Jesus, he was very glad, for
> he had long desired to see him, because he had
> heard about him, and he was hoping to see some
> sign done by him."* (Luke 23:8)

Jesus is still in the authentic healing and miracle ministry today but despises the commercialization of the supernatural!

Real miracles are common, particularly in the third world, and I don't mean to imply for a minute that all supernatural manifestations are demonic. Revivals are sloppy and strange things may occur when there is a great outpouring of the Holy Spirit. It takes great spiritual discernment to know what a work of the Holy Spirit is and what is the work of demonic spirits sent to interrupt or side track a work of God. **The mark of any true revival is contrition, humility, true repentance, and a passion for God and His word.** A review of past revivals has demonstrated strange behaviors often accompanying a true move of the Holy Spirit. It seems that Satan will do his best to discredit a true move of God with his counterfeit healings and miracles. Jonathan Edwards (1703-1758), the great revivalist of the eighteenth century and a leader in the first great American awaking of the early 1700s, wrote about his experiences in his books *Thoughts on Revival and Religious Affections.* He noted people with strange behavior during his revival meetings. He was a student of the history of past revivals, which were accompanied by a true move of the Holy Spirit and genuine repentance. They were also accompanied by strange behavior and outbursts. Many passed out and were speechless as they were convicted of their sin; others appeared to have convulsions. He simply ignored many who were excited and had aberrant behavior but were not converted or touched by the Holy Spirit. Edwards did not get sidetracked from the guidance of the Holy Spirit. He preached a very unpopular message about sin, repentance, and the certainty of eternal damnation of the lost.

Edwards identified as proof of a true conversion sorrow for sin, delight in God, newfound joy, endurance of faith in the face of adversity or tragedy, but most of all a holy life with delight in God and love for his neighbor. Like most Puritans he was suspicious of sudden conversions and waited to see if a changed life with fruit of the spirit continued with the passing of time. Unlike modern evangelists Edwards was very careful not to tell people that they were saved or give false assurance until he saw proof of genuine lasting fruit in their lives. He was the first to confess that without the passage of time he couldn't be sure of someone's salvation in spite of their claims of a great spiritual conversion experience. Unlike modern evangelicals, he recognized that the intensity of the spiritual experience was not proof of genuine conversion. He preached during the revival that many are like the seed that fell on rocky soil in Matthew 13:5-6: *"Other seeds fell on rocky ground, where they did not have much soil, and <u>immediately they sprang up</u>, since they had no depth of soil, but when the sun rose, they were scorched. And since they had no root, they withered away."* He thought that many sudden conversions were false conversions.

Edwards waited to see if the fruit was genuine and lasting and not an emotional flash in the pan. *"Whoever abides in me and I in him, he it is that bears much fruit, for apart from me you can do nothing. If anyone does not abide in me, he is thrown away like a branch and withers;"* (John 15:5-6) *"As for what was sown on good soil, this is the one who hears the word and understands it. He indeed bears fruit and yields, in one case a hundredfold, in another sixty, and in another thirty."* (Matt. 13:23)

Edwards wrote that the fruit of a true conversion was personal holiness. *"And by this we know that we have come to know him if we keep his commandments. Whoever says, "I know him" but does not keep his commandments is a liar, and the truth is not in him, but whoever keeps his word, in him truly the love of God is perfected."* (1 John 2:3-5)

The consistent mark of the fruit of true revival is the abhorrence of one's own sin, corruption, vileness, and self-loathing for it. This leads to true repentance, restitution, when possible, faith in Christ, and a life lived in *agape* love and holiness. It is the necessary knowledge of personal sin and taking responsibility for it, that brings repentance and changed behavior and a God-centered life. Revivals are full of emotion and excitement, many cry out under the conviction of the Holy Spirit and others may undergo spiritual deliverance. Jonathan Edwards kept control of his meetings and did not allow his meetings to develop into a circus sideshow. He was able to discern between false and true religious affections. He kept the focus on Jesus as Lord, Savior, and eternal judge of wickedness, and not on himself. He recognized that any conversion is the sovereign choice and work of God and not based on the preacher's cleverness or oratory excellence. How we need such men with great spiritual discernment, wisdom, and humility in leadership today.

In 1801, a second great American awaking occurred in a Cane Ridge Camp Meeting in rural Kentucky. This move of God was also accompanied by people falling down crying out to God in confession and repentance. Some people howled, fell to the ground, and had uncontrollable laughing. There was much spiritual mixture, but many showed fruit of genuine repentance and conversion and revival continued for the next thirty years.

The next great American revival was at Azusa Street in Los Angeles in 1906 following the great Welch revival in 1904. Frank Bartleman was an itinerant black pastor and the leader of this great revival and a mighty man of God. He stated that "the depth of revival will be determined exactly by the depth of the spirit of repentance and a true Pentacost will produce a mighty conviction of sin and a turning to God." How right he was and he said, **"false manifestations produce only excitement and wonder... and any work that exalts the Holy Ghost or the gifts above Jesus will finally end up in fanaticism!"** The Azusa revival continued until roughly 1915. The revival was characterized by ecstatic spiritual experiences accompanied by speaking in tongues, dramatic worship services, and inter-racial mingling. There was much criticism from traditional church leaders since the majority of participants were poor, unschooled and of mixed races and outside the more erudite church leaders felt the revival participants were ignorant and vulnerable to deception. The participants received criticism from secular media as well as Christian theologians for behaviors considered to be outrageous and unorthodox, especially at the time. Today, the revival is considered by historians to be the primary catalyst for the spread of Pentecostalism in the twentieth century. It is estimated that more than 500,000,000 people around the world are now Pentecostal. Again, there was much mixture and often poor and weak theology in these early meetings but there was also the fruit of genuine conversion to Christ for many.

Unfortunately, many pastors desire revival to grow their churches so they can drive a nicer car or move to a bigger house. Too few are willing to lay down their own ministries at the foot of the cross and cry out to God for true revival and pray, *begin with me!*

I had feared for this beautiful ship since the upper two decks had no railing and a storm was coming, and all these men could easily be swept into the sea. I knew they would quickly sink to the bottom since their pockets were filled with gold. They didn't seem to understand how slippery the decks would become when wet and that they were standing on very slippery ground. Those prophets that clung to their oars would be saved because these large wooden oars would float. In the coming great storm, their chains would be broken and their voices heard. We sailed slowly by the ship, and I asked a crewman why the ship was not moving? He explained that they were anchored to a ball of gold and could not raise the anchor because of its weight. They could not move any closer to the Promised Land unless they cut the anchor chain, which seemed unlikely unless it was broken by a great storm which was surely coming. I thought to myself, the false prophet does not fear God nor accept the council of God. When the big storms come, they will call upon God but He will not answer!

> *"Because you have ignored all my counsel and would have none of my reproof, I also will laugh at your calamity; I will mock when terror strikes you, when terror strikes you like a storm, and your calamity comes like a whirlwind, when distress and anguish come upon you. Then they will call upon me, but I will not answer; they will seek me diligently but will not find me. Because they hated knowledge and did not choose the fear of the Lord."* (Prov. 1:25-29)

I mourned at the certain sinking of this beautiful ship and wondered, where are the prophets today? In charismatic Pentecostal circles the understanding of the prophet is a person who speaks in tongues accompanied by signs and wonders such as healings, great visions, and prophetic pronouncements of future events. The modern day "prophet" is careful to avoid criticism of the hosting church or ministry. He speaks blessings wherever he goes. He may use clairvoyance or mind reading to give a personal word of something hidden in the heart of an individual. To many Pentecostal believers, the demonstration of the supernatural authenticates the prophet, rather than tested Godly character with fruit of the spirit as opposed to just the signs of the spirit.

In ancient Israel prophets for hire where part of religious practice. These men were called in Hebrew *"Nabi"* or seers during the 8th century BC era of Amos. *"Then Amos answered and said to Amaziah, "I was no prophet, nor a prophet's son, but I was a herdsman and a dresser of sycamore figs. But the Lord took me from following the flock, and the Lord said to me, 'Go, prophesy to my people Israel.' Now therefore hear the word of the Lord."* (Amos 7:14-16)

Amos denied he was a prophet *Nabi* but was a 'visionary' (Heb. *"ḥozeh"*), a title that refers to the distinctive means by which these individuals received their revelations. The distinction is made from those temple prophets for hire who may have had supernatural discernment about people and revealed their thoughts and secrets by divination as well as an interpreter of dreams and visions, or a seer, or a professional diviner like Balaam, versus the true prophet of God or *"ḥozeh"* who is not for hire and reveals the secrets of God by direct revelation from God. *"For the Lord God does nothing without revealing his secret to his servants the prophets."* (Amos 3:7) See Deuteronomy 13:1-5, 18:9-20, Jeremiah 27:9, 29:8, Ezekiel 13:2-10, and Isaiah 44:25.

God chooses to speak through broken, tested vessels who distain the applause of men and are filled with holy boldness and seek only the Glory of God. They are men of great courage like Amos who was a simple farmer. These biblical men of God endured persecutions and great trials. Paul was asked to authenticate his apostolic-prophetic ministry and he never boasted about the miracles he performed or any other works of the Spirit. He replied to those who wanted proof of his apostolic prophetic office as follows:

> *"Are they servants of Christ? I am a better one—I am talking like a madman—with far greater labors, far more imprisonments, with countless beatings, and often near death. Five times I received at the hands of the Jews the forty lashes less one. Three times I was beaten with rods. Once I was stoned. Three times I was shipwrecked; a night and a day I was adrift at sea; on frequent journeys, in danger from rivers, danger from robbers, danger from my own people, danger from Gentiles, danger in the city, danger in the wilderness, danger at sea, danger from false brothers; in toil and hardship, through many a sleepless night, in hunger and thirst, often without food, in cold and exposure. And, apart from other things, there is the daily pressure on me of my anxiety for all the churches. Who is weak, and I am not weak? Who is made to fall, and I am not indignant?"* (2 Cor. 11:23-29)

Those who claim to speak for God will endure great opposition, as did Jonathan Edwards who after conducting a mighty revival was expelled from his own church in Northampton, Massachusetts. He faced many trials and much opposition from other church leaders yet was a true prophetic spokesman for the Lord. **Many think that the primary concern of the prophet is apocalyptic or prediction of end time events concerning the Church. The primary ministry of the prophet has always been conviction of sin, preaching of repentance, judgment, and hope for salvation in God. The fruit is personal holiness and revival.**

We live in a time similar to the time of Jeremiah just prior to the destruction of Jerusalem, where there are many false prophets and corrupt priests and the people loved it.

> *"An appalling and horrible thing has happened in the land: the prophets prophesy falsely, and the priest's rule at their direction; my people love to have it so, but what will you do when the end comes?"* (Jeremiah 5:30-31)

Chapter 12

RELIGION

After passing the prophetic ship, another ship appeared over the horizon coming close to us. It was black, very large, beautiful, and covered with gold, silver, and jewels. It had as its figurehead on its bow, Mary the mother of Jesus. It was called *Religion*. It also had three large decks. The top deck was called transubstantiation. On that deck were thrones for men, popes, and prelates who gained their power by restricting access to the communion host of God, which they taught was necessary for salvation. There were many statues of Mary and various Saints adorned with gold and jewels. The Host or communion bread was kept in a gold and jewel encrusted box. The prelates ruled with absolute authority and if any man denied their power he would be thrown into the sea. There was a vast congregation, so large that it could not be counted. On the second deck priests were selling indulgences using the quotation from Tetzel: "As soon as the coin in the coffer rings, the soul from purgatory springs." And there was also a Treasury Box of Merits.

On the lowest deck there was a house of prostitution toward the bow of the ship and an elaborate confessional at the stern of the ship set in a large ring, about 150 feet in diameter, like a platter on rollers. On the side facing the bow was a most beautiful and attractive edifice, which was a house of prostitution. Over the house was a most attractive lustful sign was written; *"Idolatry, Lust of the Flesh, Love of this World, Pride of Life."* The confessional was very ornate and appeared to be set in a beautiful cathedral. Men would leave from the confessional in the cathedral and push the turntable with their feet as they walked to rotate the turntable toward the house of prostitution. These men would re-enter the house of prostitution for a time and then return to the turntable and rotate it again with their feet to the confessional so that men could confess their sins and be "forgiven" again and again. The movement of this turntable around and around drove a vertical shaft to a spur gear that connected to the horizontal propeller shaft of the ship. The movement of the turntable is called the sin cycle and powers the ship. This religious ship, in actuality, was powered by guilt, shame, fear of hell, duty, condemnation, obligation, pride, religious tradition and works, fear of man, and works of penance! It is these motivational emotions that drive all religious ships.

This sin cycle is not limited to only the Catholic Church, but any church that pronounces absolution without demanding true repentance, and not just penance. Cheap grace and cheap forgiveness perpetuate the sin cycle. Many protestant denominations also have confession followed by absolution in their liturgy. There can never be true forgives without confession of sin followed by true repentance. Church leaders who pronounce absolution of sin without demanding repentance perpetuate the sin cycle that drives theses religious ships.

The lay people in this religious ship were told that the church leaders had the actual body and blood of Christ when they blessed the communion elements. Men were told that if they would partake of such communion Mass and confession that they would be saved as long as the came back and did it again and again. The church's dogma and tradition overruled and subordinated the Scriptures. There was no need to read the Bible since they were told they couldn't understand it anyway, and that all the knowledge needed for salvation could be learned by attending their church. The reformers spoke of the churches devocalizing God by not allowing Him to speak through His Word. The reformation was all about letting God speak through His Word rather than church prelates and councils. The reformers insisted that the Bible be translated in the local language and that church services be conducted not in Latin, but the local language. This produced the Protestant revolution of a personal God who speaks to every man through His Word, the Bible.

Religious people often interpret the Bible through church tradition, councils, and words of church prelates and popes instead of allowing the Bible to interpret itself. This is the deification of fallible human authority. All religions except Biblical Christianity espouse salvation by works or faith and works. True Christianity is centered on salvation by faith alone and not works. Works will always follow those who are born again but are not a condition of salvation. "Justification is by faith alone, but not by faith that is alone." Those that deny justification by faith alone are denying the sufficiency of Christ's atonement! It is a very dangerous thing to add to the completed work of Christ.

Many of us have had precious friends whom we love dearly that attend various types of Religious Ships. It has always amazed me how difficult it is to know the true spiritual condition of religious people. Some are wheat and some are tares. It is only when the grain is ready for harvest that the wheat and tares can be separated. We may never know the answer to this question in this life. We will have to await until the final harvest according to Matthew's gospel.

> *"The kingdom of heaven may be compared to a man who sowed good seed in his field, but while his men were sleeping, his enemy came and sowed weeds among the wheat and went away. So when the plants came up and bore grain, then the weeds appeared also. And the servants of the master of the house came and said to him, 'Master, did you not sow good seed in your field? How then does it have weeds?' He said to them, 'An enemy has done this.' So the servants said to him, 'Then do*

*you want us to go and gather them?' But he said,
'No, lest in gathering the weeds you root up the
wheat along with them. Let both grow together
until the harvest, and at harvest time I will tell the
reapers, Gather the weeds first and bind them in
bundles to be burned, but gather the wheat into
my barn.'"* (Matt. 13:24-30)

We must be careful to be guided by the
Holy Spirit's discernment. *"Not that we dare to
classify or compare ourselves with some of those
who are commending themselves. But when they
measure themselves by one another and compare
themselves with one another, they are without
understanding."* (2 Cor. 10:12) and *"Let the one
who boasts, boast in the Lord."* For it is not the one
who commends himself who is approved, but the
one whom the Lord commends."* (2 Cor. 10:17)

The weather was changing, and the seas were becoming
larger. There was so much weight on the top deck because of all
the gold and jewels; I knew that in a matter of time the ship would
become unstable and flip over and all would be lost because it was
so top heavy.

**Another ship came into view that was very modest in
appearance and somber looking. It had no significant decoration
and appeared to be very functional and ready for any storms
ahead. It was called** *Reformation.* **On the deck of the ship were
men in peaceful disputation. They were arguing different points
of theology. Some believed that the instruments of Communion
were not an empty sign, but very spiritual, others shouted NO!
They felt that communion was an instrument of grace placed in
his church to feed his church physically and spiritually. Others
emphatically disagreed and thought that communion was a sign
of grace but not an instrument through which a believer was
sanctified. Communion was to them a testimony of the work
of Christ and largely symbolic and not an instrument of grace.**

These somber men continued to argue with intensity. Suddenly there arose a man who stood up and grabbed the bullhorn and said to all the men that they must humble themselves since they would be hearing from the Master Himself as to the fine points of theology.

Christ would explain all things soon and was but a short distance away through uncharted waters. The men were encouraged to stop disputing various theological issues and focus on trying to see the biblical perspective and make peace. The speaker pointed out that it was a much greater sin not to love one's brother than to be theologically correct. He encouraged the men to agree on the essentials of the faith including salvation by grace alone, justification by faith alone, and not by works, Christ alone as our hope, atonement, and source of all things, the authority of scripture, the resurrection, and eternal punishment of the wicked that all things be for the Glory of God alone.

It was the perfect work of Christ on the cross for the forgiveness of sins that had purchased our salvation and brought the indwelling of the Holy Spirit for sanctification, and the hope of His return to rule the earth that brought hope to men. All agreed that the purpose of life was to glorify God and to advance the Kingdom of God. They agreed with the Apostles and Nicene creeds yet disputed many issues such as baptism.

Suddenly the men began to weep as the Holy Spirit opened their eyes and they saw the divisiveness caused by their sectarianism and denominationalism. The speaker pointed out that this was the result of pride, arrogance, and a party spirit. He pointed out that diversities of understanding, theology, and church practice are to be tolerated but never divided, as long as they conform to the basic foundations of biblical Christ-centered faith. If Christ is the center of His church, then the focus should be on the essentials of the faith and not on any issue that would separate the body. The speaker pointed out that when Christ is not the center many issues will come forth that will divide his church. Division shows our lack of true spirituality and is not pleasing to the Lord. Therefore, Paul called the men to repent of their divisiveness and the party spirit, which was a sin of the flesh and repugnant to God. The captain of the ship came forward and announced that there were great storms ahead and he doubted the ship would survive unless there was unity as well as the celebration of diversity in the ship. Each man was called to his station and life preservers were passed out in case the ship floundered.

Chapter 13

DENOMINATIONALISM

I had encountered a ship called *"Denomination"* from the Religious Cruise line. The Religious Cruise Line ships were noted to be high sided and very rigid. Some of these religious ships were decorated and embellished with decorations and gold and others were very plain. The *"Denomination"* was a very religious ship that required people to obey certain rules if they were to stay on the ship. The leaders focused on the differences in their group from others so that it made their group seem superior. This enabled man to feel better about themselves and have what they thought was increased self-worth because they were part of a group that had the correct understanding of Scripture. It was part of a huge fleet of more than 35,000 different denominational ships. In the center of this ship was a large boxing ring. Two men were boxing, one called Exclusiveness and the other Inclusiveness. The referee was called Scripture but both boxers were pummeling him. He was beaten so badly that the referee called Scripture became barely recognizable.

Richard Niebuhr commented "denominationalism represents the moral failure of Christianity." That is a very strong statement, but denominationalism reflects poorly to an outside world examining critically examining our Christian faith. How do denominations begin? Generally, denominations are formed by groups of men hoping to encapsulate a recent move of the Holy Spirit that has already passed. They are composed of like-minded people with common beliefs and objectives. A denomination does not claim to be the church but a partial manifestation of the church. Once religion is a private affair people feel free to associate with like-minded people and move from denomination to denomination. This makes denominationalism a very Western and American practice reflecting the American independent spirit.

God spoke strongly to Jeremiah about religious spirit that focuses on the past move of God rather than the present. God calls the desertion of the living water, or what God was currently doing in his church, EVIL! The Jewish leaders of that day where stuck in empty formalities and practices that once had great meaning and had missed the river of living water.

> *"For my people have committed two evils: they have forsaken me, the fountain of living waters, and hewed out cisterns for themselves, broken cisterns that can hold no water." (Jeremiah 2:13)*

God is ever-present and His Spirit is continuously flowing as a fountain of living water into His Church. His revelation is "new every morning." Denominations are just leaky cisterns hoping to contain the past move of the Spirit of God. These cisterns are filled with stale water that cannot relieve the thirsty soul. They are focused more on what God did than what is God doing. The freshness of His spirit is to be sought continuously since it cannot be captured by the devices or works of man! We are to live by what the Spirit is doing today, rather than in the past moves of God.

Notice that it is only fresh water, flowing water, or living water, a metaphor for the Holy Spirit, that cleans us from sin. Water stored in cisterns could not be used by the priest to cleanse the leper (Sinners like us) since it was not fresh flowing water.

> *"The Lord spoke to Moses, saying, "This shall be the law of the leprous person for the day of his cleansing. He shall be brought to the priest, and*

the priest shall go out of the camp, and the priest shall look. Then, if the case of leprous disease is healed in the leprous person, the priest shall command them to take for him who is to be cleansed two live clean birds and cedarwood and scarlet yarn and hyssop. And the priest shall command them to kill one of the birds in an earthenware vessel over fresh water (in Hebrew running water from a stream). He shall take the live bird with the cedarwood and the scarlet yarn and the hyssop, and dip them and the live bird in the blood of the bird that was killed over the fresh water. And he shall sprinkle it seven times on him who is to be cleansed of the leprous disease. Then he shall pronounce him clean and shall let the living bird go into the open field." (Leviticus 14:1-7)

We must be careful to seek and move with the Holy Spirit of God, the spring of living water, not building, or relying on empty leaky cisterns filled with stale water; yet never compromising foundational truth.

The value of a denomination has been the maintenance of orthodoxy, but often the focus becomes church tradition and knowing doctrine and the bible above knowing the God of the bible. Many books are written about the need of the church to look outward rather than just inward. Few are written encouraging the church to look upward to the fountain of living water.

To the non-Christian world, and also for many Christians the lack of unity in the church is deplorable. If we are to love our brother, why can't we agree on the essentials and get along? This is not a new problem but began in the first century in the Corinthian church. Paul pleaded:

"I appeal to you, brothers, by the name of our Lord Jesus Christ, that all of you agree, and that there be no divisions among you, but that you be united in the same mind and the same judgment. For it has been reported to me by Chloe's people that there is quarreling among

you, my brothers. What I mean is that each one of you says, "I follow Paul," or "I follow Apollos," or "I follow Cephas," or "I follow Christ." Is Christ divided?" (1 Cor. 1:12-13)

Now there are more than 35,000 Christian denominations! Christians may disagree over secondary issues but are never to disagree over the primary foundations of the faith. Unfortunately, many leaders don't know what these essential beliefs are! Too many are biblically ignorant. Many Christian organizations are willing to sacrifice basic essential doctrine for purposes of unity. This *Deeds over Creeds* or *one big tent where everyone is welcome* type of unity is unbiblical.

An obscure ancient seventeenth century theologian named Rupertus Meldenius wisely penned the phrase: **"In essentials unity, in non-essentials liberty, and in all things charity."** The five primary essentials of Christ alone, grace alone, faith alone, His glory alone, and Scripture alone never change. Unity requires agreement on essential, sound biblical doctrines such as the Trinity, the Deity and Humanity of Christ, justification by grace alone through faith alone, the eternal judgment of the wicked, the authority of Scripture, the penal substitutionary atonement of Christ on the cross followed by His resurrection from the dead, and most of all the exclusivity and efficacy of salvation through faith in Christ alone. Inherent in basic doctrine is the requirement of holiness and obedience. Doctrine produces boundaries, which have always been a source of struggle for the church. Secondary issues such as child baptism, eschatology, election, and use of the gifts of the spirit may cause separation into different fellowships, based on secondary doctrines, but hopefully always maintaining bonds of love and fellowship toward our brothers who also agree on the primary essentials. If our priority is living for Christ and building His kingdom we can love and fellowship with those with whom we disagree. Paul expressly speaks to all of us about judging our brother over non-essential issues.

> *"As for the one who is weak in faith, welcome him, but not to quarrel over opinions. One person believes he may eat anything, while the weak*

person eats only vegetables. Let not the one who eats despise the one who abstains and let not the one who abstains pass judgment on the one who eats, for God has welcomed him. Who are you to pass judgment on the servant of another? It is before his own master that he stands or falls. And he will be upheld, for the Lord is able to make him stand. One person esteems one day as better than another, while another esteems all days alike. Each one should be fully convinced in his own mind. The one who observes the day, observes it in honor of the Lord. The one who eats, eats in honor of the Lord, since he gives thanks to God, while the one who abstains, abstains in honor of the Lord, and gives thanks to God. For none of us lives to himself, and none of us dies to himself. For if we live, we live to the Lord, and if we die, we die to the Lord. So then, whether we live or whether we die, we are the Lord's. For to this end Christ died and lived again, that he might be Lord both of the dead and of the living. Why do you pass judgment on your brother? Or you, why do you despise your brother? For we will all stand before the judgment seat of God; for it is written, "As I live, says the Lord, every knee shall bow to me, and every tongue shall confess to God." So then each of us will give an account of himself to God. Therefore, let us not pass judgment on one another any longer, but rather decide never to put a stumbling block or hindrance in the way of a brother." (Rom. 14:1-13)

Third order essentials such as debates over issues, like whether women should have their heads covered in church (I Corinthians 11:5), should never separate us from our brother. In the book of First John, the foundation and emphasis of *koinonea* or Christian fellowship is walking in the light, in truth, and obedience, with transparency and love. (1 John 1:5-10) When we examine these verses in First John we can't help but see The Lord's passion for our walking out our faith in light, unity, and truth. John was speaking about the invisible community of all true believers in a day before there were institutional churches. The later development of doctrinal churches has brought conflicting allegiances to the local church versus the overall community of believers.

The purpose of good theology is to equip the saints to walk out their faith in truth and to protect us from deception! Sound theology by its very nature produces boundaries. Good sound theology without a life lived in biblical obedience is pure hypocrisy and brings scandal to the church. Good sound biblical doctrine is the framework upon which we build our understanding of God and always glorifies God and not man. Our doctrine frames our worldview, attitudes, and behavior. Our correct biblical doctrine protects us from heresy and false beliefs. Our theology is extremely important but doesn't save us. It is our fellowship with Christ in obedience and love that saves us *"that I know Him."* When we arrive at the gate of Heaven, perhaps Jesus' only question is *do I know you or know you not?* (present tense) Many claim to have known Him (past tense) in the past but are not currently in relationship with Him and do not know Him now. No angelic being is going to ask us any questions about what church or fellowship we attended or our theological position on issues.

> *"But if we walk in the light, as He is in the light, we have fellowship with one another, and the blood of Jesus his Son cleanses us from all sin. If we say we have no sin, we deceive ourselves, and the truth is not in us. If we confess our sins, He is faithful and just to forgive us our sins and to cleanse us from all unrighteousness. If we say we have not sinned, we make him a liar, and His Word is not in us."* (1 John 1:7-10)

> *"And by this we know that we have come to know Him if we keep His commandments. Whoever says "I know Him" but does not keep His commandments is a liar, and the truth is not in him, but whoever keeps His Word, in him truly the love of God is perfected. By this we may know that we are in Him: whoever says he abides in Him ought to walk in the same way in which He walked." (1 John 2:3-6)*

Hugh Latimer, the great English reformer, who was burned at the stake at Oxford in 1555 by Catholic Queen Mary because of his reformed Protestant views, said: ***"We ought never regard unity so much that we would or should forsake God's word for her sake."*** Sound doctrine necessarily separates and can never be compromised for the sake of unity. It also unifies. Forced unity squelches personal differences and results in forced conformity. This saps the life out of man and binds the Spirit. Unity by the Spirit is based on the unfolding revelation of God through study of His Word. If we love God, we will love our brothers and sisters. Doctrinal issues are important, but except for the fundamental essential issues, they are not an excuse for divisions and a party spirit.

> *"Whoever says he is in the light and hates his brother is still in darkness. Whoever loves his brother abides in the light, and in him there is no cause for stumbling. But whoever hates his brother is in the darkness and walks in the darkness, and does not know where he is going, because the darkness has blinded his eyes." (1 John 2:9-11)*

I think that, in part, the problem of denominationalism often arises from the use of the word ***Church***, which originates from the Old English *Cir(i)ce*, the Dutch *Kirk* and the German *Kirche* and which apparently is derived from the Greek *Kuriaken* or the "Lord's House." The Greek word used in the New Testament often incor-rectly translated as church is *ekklesia* and when properly translated means "called out ones, assembly, gathering, congregation, or community." King James of England gave specific instructions to the authors of the King James 1611 version of the Bible to use the word "Church" rather than assembly or congregation. The church authorities in England were very concerned about any Bible translation that might undermine their authority. The word Church separates and produces a party spirit because it implies separation into different groups or denominations such as Baptists, Methodists, and Presbyterians etc. It also implies that there is only one "right denomination" such as the Church of England. The word in common usage implies that denominationalism is normative rather than an inexcusable fundamental sin. Paul makes it abundantly clear that there is only *one body*, which is not confined to any particular sect, denomination, or religious party.

> *"I therefore, a prisoner for the Lord, urge you to walk in a manner worthy of the calling to which you have been called, with all humility and gentleness, with patience, bearing with one another in love, <u>eager to maintain the unity of the Spirit in the bond of peace. There is* **one body** *and one Spirit—just as you were called to the one hope that belongs to your call one Lord, one faith, one baptism, one God and Father of all, who is over all and through all and in all</u>."* (Eph. 4:1-6)

Denominationalism often produces and encourages a religious spirit, which God hates. Religion is the effort of man to produce his own righteousness, thinking it is pleasing to God. It implies that man can add something to the righteousness of Christ, which was purchased on the cross for all men forever. Religious works blaspheme the finished work of God. The religious spirit produces pride, arrogance, and a sense of superiority, which blinds men to their own sin. Paul said to the Galatians:

> *"O foolish Galatians! Who has bewitched you? It
> was before your eyes that Jesus Christ was pub-
> licly portrayed as crucified. Let me ask you only
> this: Did you receive the Spirit by works of the
> law or by hearing with faith? Are you so foolish?
> Having begun by the Spirit, are you now being
> perfected by the flesh?"* (Gal. 3:1-3)

Many churches promote "a particular church membership"
which is absolutely unbiblical. Prior to the reformation and the
enlightenment, the church era was called the *"Corpus Christianum"*
in that there were no divisions. Biblical is membership in the whole
body of Christ is via confession of sin followed by repentance and
baptism followed by receiving the Holy Spirit, as described in Acts
2:37-39:

*"Now when they heard this they were cut to the heart, and said
to Peter and the rest of the apostles, "Brothers, what shall we do?"
And Peter said to them, "Repent and be baptized every one of you
in the name of Jesus Christ for the forgiveness of your sins, and you
will receive the gift of the Holy Spirit. **For the promise is for you and
for your children and <u>for all</u> who are far off, everyone whom the Lord
our God calls to himself"***

There is only one church and that is composed of all believers.
Partisan religious groups promote church membership in an effort
to control the congregation under the guise of protecting the saints
from false doctrine and spiritual predators. This motive seems worthy but in fact is often used to keep control, prevent dissention, limit
decision making to "only members in good standing," and to prevent any questioning of church authority or dogma. This practice
of "it's our way or the highway" is very self-serving and hurts the
church by limiting creativity, biblical correction, and the leading by
the Holy Spirit. The practice of inclusiveness through church membership often brings unwanted exclusiveness and false pride.

The biblical model is that assemblies or congregations are to be established in communities

and limited by primarily geographic boundaries with ruling elders. Membership was of God's choosing in that all called of God and who were repentant and born again were included. *"Our citizenship is in heaven."* (Phil. 3:20) By promoting church membership based on anything other than God's sovereign election, we reinforce the error of denominationalism. *"So we, though many, are one body in Christ, and individually members one of another."* (Rom. 12:5)

"Or just as the body is one and has many members, and all the members of the body, though many, are one body, so it is with Christ. For in one Spirit, we were all baptized into one body—Jews or Greeks, slaves or free—and all were made to drink of one Spirit." (1 Cor. 12:12-13)

There was another cruise line called *"The Independent Church Cruise Line."* They had similar views and rules as the Denominational Cruise Line and also felt superior because they had a better grasp of the truth and correct doctrine. They had many more ships then the denominational cruise line. These ships were often focused on a leader rather than doctrine. These churches were often filled with people who are uncomfortable in many churches and simply didn't feel they had any place else to go. They didn't feel they fit into any religious system. They often stayed because they couldn't find anything else. Unfortunately, many church leaders were more interested in building their own little kingdoms then in building the Kingdom of God!

Often the independent churches are equally guilty of the sin of arrogance in that they fail to discern the body of Christ. They may be led by great teachers and enjoy being exclusive rather than inclusive and sharing and caring for the whole body of Christ. Paul spoke to the Corinthians about some which were more concerned about themselves rather than the body as a whole when they shared communion.

"Whoever, therefore, eats the bread or drinks the cup of the Lord in an unworthy manner will be guilty concerning the body and blood of the Lord. Let a person examine himself, then, and so eat of the bread and drink of the cup. For anyone who eats and drinks without discerning the body eats and drinks judgment on himself. That is why many of you are weak and ill, and some have died. But if we judged ourselves truly, we would not be judged. But when we are judged by the Lord, we are disciplined so that we may not be condemned along with the world." (1 Cor. 11:27-32)

Notice the emphasis Paul puts on sharing communion in an *unworthy manor*. The failure to discern the body of Christ is very serious and many Christians are sick, weak, and ill. Some have died for failure to discern the body of Christ!! A pride filled leader may use right doctrine in an arrogant manor to exalt himself, which causes division and controversy. This is never acceptable and is a serious sin. The battle of the cultural war that is upon us requires collaboration without doctrinal compromise. I have seen denominational differences melt away as the church comes together to fight a common enemy. The increasing pressure to marginalize Christianity is breaking the bonds of the denominational spirit. We need each other! There always will be disagreement between some Christians over minor issues such as the role of women in the church. We always must disagree in love when necessary. Doctrine by its very nature divides. Jesus taught that He did not come to bring peace on earth but division in Luke 12:51-53, and Matthew 10:34-38. The division He spoke about was primarily about the Christian disciple versus the world. Our enemy is the world system and not our brother. Paul reminds us, *"not to seek our own, but each others well-being."* (I Corinthians 10:24) Doctrine may produce controversy but we are told to avoid foolish controversies. (I Timothy 1:4-6; 4:7; 6:4,20; 2 Timothy 2:14,16, 23; 4:4) Doctrinal issues should always be discussed in an atmosphere of love. We must rely on the inspiration of the Holy Spirit to be the referee between brothers with different understandings of scripture. Ultimately, church fathers, church creeds, and the teaching of the reformers, Puritan divines, and other great men of God will help guide us in understanding correct doctrine. We recognize that, "all synods or councils, since apostolic times, whether general or particular, may err; and may have erred." (Westminster Confession of Faith 31:3) Scripture is the ultimate authority.

Foundational doctrine can never be compromised since doctrine and practice cannot be separated. Bad doctrine results in moral compromise. Many church leaders search for the center in theological discussions. There can be no center for discussion unless there is agreement on the theological boundaries. It is these boundaries that determine the center. Doctrine divides and unfortunately for many, doctrine becomes the sole basis of fellowship. We don't have to change or compromise our doctrine to fellowship with a Christian brother with different doctrinal beliefs. A healthy congregation or assembly looks to Christ first and foremost and teaches men the bible, which if properly taught, always will teach good doctrine. There should be no attempt to teach good doctrine and not the bible. A healthy assembly will also teach and equip men to know and be led by the Holy Spirit and to love their brother.

Christ's last prayer in John 17:22-23 was that there be unity in the church: " *The glory that you have given me I have given to them, that they may be one even as we are one, I in them and you in me, that they may become perfectly one, so that the world may know that you sent me and loved them even as you loved me.*"

Our witness to the world is unity, without compromise, around the essentials of Christian doctrine and liberty on minor issues and: "*If possible, so far as it depends on you, live peaceably with all.*" (Romans 12:18)

Chapter 14

FUNDALMENTALISM

Late that evening a very plain looking high-sided rigid ship came into view. This was the ship *Hypocritical*. It was part of the Fundamentalist Fleet that included several other ships called Judgments, Prejudice, Parochialism, Gossip, Religious Superiority, Anti-intellectualism, Religious Spirit, Legalism, Phony Baloney, Righteous and Rowdy, the Do's and the Don'ts, and many others. It was interesting as I observed the leadership in the various vessels that when they were close to each other, they did not exchange greetings or signals. I noted that the people on the upper decks were very formally dressed in suits and dresses. They all wore white hats. The music was somber, and they all carried large black Chart Books. Others were dressed as ordinary seamen and scurried about polishing the brass, washing windows, and cleaning the ship. The leaders spoke against sin and seemed very righteous. Since it was almost night, I could see below decks and the people were drinking, taking drugs, and there was a lot of sexual activity. The people looked guilty and rushed to close their blinds on their staterooms once they realized they had been discovered.

I asked the mate about this group of fundamental ships, and he explained they put their hope in their religious pietistic actions and outward behavior. They focused on doing some-

thing for God. In Romans 10:2 Paul describes many of these people with a works mentality:

> *"They have a zeal for God, but not according to knowledge. For, being ignorant of the righteousness of God, and seeking to establish their own, they did not submit to God's righteousness. For Christ is the end of the law for righteousness to everyone who believes."*

Many were cultural Christians and grew up in a similar ship. They were strong believers in the Christian ethic, family, and their cultural values. Their hope was in their works of piety, morality, and faith in Jesus. It reminded me of Martin Luther's words: *"God does not need your good works, your neighbor does."* They believed that the Chart Book was the Word of God, but most had never read the book or met the author, the Master Mariner. Their Chart Book was like their cookbook. It had all the answers, and no critical thinking was allowed or necessary since the leaders had all the answers on how to interpret the cookbook. Intellectual dissent was not to be tolerated or encouraged. Their biblical hermeneutic was that the Bible was to be taken literally and was factually inerrant about facts not only of faith, but also of science, nature, and history. They knew all about Him and worshiped Him but did not have the power of the Holy Spirit. The law was often a vehicle of regulation rather than revelation. They tried to obey the Chart Book but lacked the power to obey. They criticized the other ships, which just like them were also cruising in circles, and wearing black hats, not white hats like they did, and also for never making any progress towards the Promised Land.

The Holiness movement in the late nineteenth and early twentieth centuries placed emphasis on outward holiness and piety such as avoiding alcoholic beverages, immodest dress, fancy clothes, dancing, card playing, gambling, theater or movies, cosmetics for women, and elaborate hair styles. It has been a failure since true holiness begins with a loving heart relationship with Christ. Holiness works outwardly from within a man and not inwardly from outward behavior. Legalism or Pietism does not bring inward change.

> *"And the word of the Lord will be to them precept upon precept, precept upon precept, line upon line, line upon line, here a little, there a little, that they may go, and fall backward, and be broken, and snared, and taken."* (Isa. 28:13)

The mate commented that many who study the Chart Book become legalistic, proud, arrogant, and self-righteousness. He stated that head knowledge often produces pride, but heart knowledge produces humility. Andrew Murray wrote in his book *Humility*: *"The chief mark of counterfeit holiness is its lack of humility."*

So many men studied the Chart Book and have never met the author. To them the author is a historical figure rather than a personal savior. They claim to be born again but forget that you can't be born again without death of self. Most men are not willing to pay the cost of becoming a disciple of the Master Mariner.

They forget that true conversion is not just a decision for the Master made by a simple showing of hands but a life that is laid down at the foot of the cross. It is an exchanged life where there is death to the old man in exchange for new life in Christ. There can be no compromise. Men forget that we cannot have one foot in the world and one foot in the Kingdom of God. The Master promises to be committed only to those who are truly committed to Him by grace and grace alone and not by works. These people believed not only in *salvation by works* but *salvation by appearance*. Their focus was on the externals and keeping the rules rather than the internals. They have been largely unprepared for the incursion of secular humanism, particularly among the youth of today. Unfortunately, a theistic moralism is unable to deal with the root problem of sin. Some of these men will call out to Jesus and He will say:

> *"Not everyone who says to me, 'Lord, Lord,' will enter the kingdom of heaven, but the one who does the will of my Father who is in heaven. On that day many will say to me, 'Lord, Lord, did we not prophesy in your name, and cast out demons in your name, and do many mighty works in your name?' And then will I declare to them, 'I never knew you; depart from me, you workers of lawlessness."* (Matt. 7:21-23)

Jesus, the Master Mariner, reminds us that the world knows us by our love for one another rather than our religious works.

> *"A new commandment I give to you, that you love one another: just as I have loved you, you also are to love one another. By this all people will know that you are my disciples, if you have love for one another."* (John 13:34-35)

Love is the fulfilling of the law!

> *"Owe no one anything, except to love each other, for he one who loves another has fulfilled the law. For the commandments, "You shall not commit adultery, you shall not murder, You shall not steal, You shall not covet," and any other commandment, are summed up in this word: "You shall love your neighbor as yourself." Love does no wrong to a neighbor; <u>therefore, love is the fulfilling of the law</u>."* (Rom. 13:8-10)

God's Love is not blind to sin or deception and makes no excuses for it. To love my neighbor as myself is to see him as a sinner like myself in deep need of redemption by God. It is to pray for others recognizing that mankind's condition is hopeless unless God sovereignly saves him. I can do nothing to save my neighbor except demonstrate God's love and when words are necessary tell him about the saving work of Jesus on the cross. We try to show the kindness and mercy of God to others hoping that they will see the goodness and kindness of our Savior and come under the conviction of God for their sin and seek confession and repentance. Our greatest witness for Christ is a life lived in joy and obedience to His Word.

Chapter 15

CHASING THE MIRACULOUS

Later, another ship came into view that was covered with flashing lights and was a very large and beautiful ship called "*Expect a Miracle*" from Pergamum, Turkey. This was another ship from the Prosperity Cruise Line. The ship had a very large amphitheater and an open stage. It was crowded with people. The main speaker wore a white suit and spoke with bold promises for healing and miracles. The crowd was very emotional and had been worked into a frenzy of expectation. Miracle workers carefully screened those who claimed a healing or miracle. They selected those who would give a testimony to come up in front to stand before the leader. This produced more excitement and anticipation for what were called manifestations of the Holy Spirit. These manifestations included violent jerking and uncontrollable laughter. There were also bodily contortions, the appearance of drunkenness, angelic encounters, and fainting in the spirit. The leader would touch various people on the forehead, and they would fall backwards and often lie motionless on the floor for several minutes. They called this being slain in the spirit. Unfortunately, many Christians are so hungry for revival and hungry to feel the touch of God that they flock to these so-called "revival meetings." These people have confused physical manifestations with a move of the Holy Spirit.

Below decks were men closely resembling Buddhist monks moaning and praying. Others wore turbans and appeared to be Hindu members of Kundalini and Shakti sects. In China they are known as "quigong." These Hindu and Buddhist mystic gurus, called Darshan, have learned how to enter the demonic world and practice demonic manifestations similar to what Christians think come from the Holy Spirit called Kriyas. These manifestations are similar or often identical to those seen in "Christian Revival Meetings with Signs and Wonders." Millions of people in Asia have experienced "this non-Christian Anointing" and have had a variety of physical and emotional experiences similar to what are thought to be manifestations of the Holy Spirit but are actual demonic manifestations. These manifestations include falling under the power of the spirit, speaking in tongues, prophetic speech and visions, barking like dogs, uncontrollable laughter, ecstatic dancing, miracles, and healings. 6

Satan is a copycat and a master counterfeiter. He has his counterfeit for every miracle, sign, or wonder from God. Unfortunately, many Christians are naive and think that whatever is supernatural must come from God. They have not been taught to distinguish between what is from the demonic and that which is from the Holy Spirit!

> *"The coming of the lawless one is by the activity of Satan with all power and false signs and wonders, and with all wicked deception for those who are perishing, because they refused to love the truth and so be saved. Therefore, God sends them a strong delusion, so that they may believe what is false, in order that all may be condemned who did not believe the truth but had pleasure in unrighteousness."* (2 Thess. 2:9-12)

---

6 For more information please read *Kundalini Warning* by Andrew Strom available at revivalschool.com or Amazon.com Please check out this video clip by Andrew Strom about true Kundalini experiences. [http://www. youtube. com/watch?v=eBp2oQrvMM]

I don't want in any way to imply that God is not also moving through the gifts of the Holy Spirit. Christians need to discern whether a supernatural manifestation is a delusion from Satan or a miracle from God! Most Christians associate revival with great signs and wonders from God. They expect a show of His power accompanied with excitement and an outpouring of his spirit like Pentecost. **True revival is about repentance and conviction of sin rather than signs and wonders. When our hearts are broken for our sin and we cry out to God for mercy, then that is revival!**

There was a constant buzz in the middle deck from this group of occultist priests as they prayed their mantras for power from the spirit world. These men gave power to the leader in the white suit.

Below the middle deck were men on the lower deck counting money. There were large sums of gold and cash, and the tables were filled with gold and silver and all types of treasures. They also worshiped the demonic spirit called Mammon, the demonic prince over wealth.

The Bible expressly warns us that in the last days there will be seducing spirits, false prophets, and lying signs and wonders. Many Christians are looking for a physical/emotional experience with God or spiritual high or fix. They travel from meeting to meeting to get their fix! The Word tells us to *"seek first the Kingdom of God and His righteousness,"* (Matt. 6:33) and not an emotional experience. We are to test the spirits and be discerning.

Man, since the time of the Tower of Babel, has sought to find power to *"make a name for ourselves,"* (Gen. 11:4). Man wants to be enthroned on earth and replace God by becoming a little god. Many of the cults promise to make their followers "little gods." Ancient people have for generations looked to the power of the occult to become as God, omniscient; able to see the future, to interpret omens, tell fortunes, and inquire of the dead. Occultist practices are absolutely forbidden for Christians but are often practiced in ignorance of Scripture.

"When you come into the land that the Lord your God is giving you, you shall not learn to follow the abominable practices of those nations. There shall not be found among you anyone who burns his son or his daughter as an offering, anyone who practices divination or tells fortunes or interprets omens, or a sorcerer or a charmer or a medium or a necromancer or one who inquires of the dead, for whoever does these things is an abomination to the Lord. And because of these abominations the Lord your God is driving them out before you. You shall be blameless before the Lord your God, for these nations, which you are about to dispossess, listen to fortune-tellers and to diviners. But as for you, the Lord your God has not allowed you to do this." (Deut. 18:9-14)

We live in a day of strong satanic delusions. We must guard our hearts and minds from the occult and focus on the truth of Scripture. It is the truth that will set us free. Americans pride themselves on being very pragmatic. We only believe what we have experienced and forget that Satan commonly uses supernatural spiritual experiences such as filling teeth with gold, gold flecks on faces, odors, feathers, being slain in the spirit, holy laughter, shaking, goose bumps, strange feelings and visions, and other devices to deceive the saints. The measure of truth is Scripture illuminated by the Holy Spirit.

"If you abide in my word, you are truly my disciples, and you will know the truth, and the truth will set you free." (John 8:31-32)

"For the word of God is living and active, sharper than any two-edged sword, piercing to the division of soul and of spirit, of joints and of marrow, and discerning the thoughts and intentions of the heart. And no creature is hidden

from his sight, but all are naked and exposed to
the eyes of him to whom we must give account."
(Heb. 4:12-13)

These prosperity teachers teach a different gospel, God becomes a small god manipulated by men, and you become as God and create your own destiny plus health, wealth and success. The secret of success is how to manipulate God to get what you want! These false teachers teach that man can create by his own faith, visualization techniques, special prayers, speaking and confessing faith (positive confession), and internal power, which is actually using the techniques of Shamanism and witchcraft. These prosperity teachers attract vulnerable, unregenerate, and lazy men who are looking for an easy way to acquire wealth shrouded in a covering of Christian speech that brings the leader great personal wealth.

God is sovereign over all and in His wisdom distributes His blessings to whom He wills! Be content with what you have and do not covet.

> *"Blessed are you, O Lord, the God of Israel our father, forever and ever. Yours, O Lord, is the greatness and the power and the glory and the victory and the majesty, for all that is in the heavens and in the earth is yours. Yours is the kingdom, O Lord, and you are exalted as head above all. Both riches and honor come from you, and you rule overall. In your hand are power and might, and in your hand, it is to make great and to give strength to all. And now we thank you, our God, and praise your glorious name. ...For all things come from you, and of your own have we given you. For we are strangers before you and sojourners, as all our fathers were. Our days on the earth are like a shadow, and there is no abiding." (1 Chron. 29:11-15)*

Chapter 16

THE SUBTLETY OF THE OCCULT

A new ship suddenly appeared on the horizon. It was very sleek and ran silently. It was called the *Deception* from the Carnal Cruise Line and also from Pergamum, Turkey where "Satan's throne is!" (Rev. 2:13). It ran on soul power and used a long snake like tail extending many yards from the stern of the ship to move forward. The bow looked like an oriental dragon. It was decorated in an oriental motif and had been built in an Asian shipyard. The back of the top deck was flat like an aircraft carrier. People were arriving and leaving on magic carpets. It had no radar. Instead, a man with white pants and no shirt, wearing a turban sat cross-legged on top of the pilothouse forecasting the future storms and hazards. There was a small observatory behind the pilothouse where astrologers were making observations. There was a psychic Captain who used clairvoyance, astrology, and mental telepathy to guide the ship. This was the latest in Christian cruise ships and ran entirely by "the latent power of the soul."

Below the top deck people were doing séances and playing with Ouija boards. Others were doing fortune telling, divination, necromancy, palm reading, and snake charming. I noted that no food was served! All these things were openly practiced as if God didn't see or forbid all these things!! Everyone must have been fasting and they all seemed very serious and many were practicing mystical meditation to hear guidance from the demons of the spirit world.

Below the main deck people were sleeping on beds of nails, doing yoga, or doing transcendental meditation, calling out their mantra. Each mantra was unique and was the name of a Hindu god or demon. The bottom deck was the teaching deck where people could learn the secrets of the occult. Many were in a hypnotic trance. Others were learning the methods of para-psychology such as mind reading, mental telepathy, palm reading, reading tea leaves and tarot cards, performing séances, and crystal ball gazing in order to divine the future. There was much money to be made in Christian prophetic circles with these gifts. The dark science of manipulation through witchcraft and cursing was very popular with long lines of people waiting to get into those classes.

My first reaction was one of horror that Christians could be involved in the occult.

> *"When you come into the land that the Lord your God is giving you, you shall not learn to follow the abominable practices of those nations. There shall not be found among you anyone who burns his son or his daughter as an offering, anyone who practices divination or tells fortunes or interprets omens, or a sorcerer or a charmer or a medium or a necromancer or one who inquires of the dead, for whoever does these things is an abomination to the Lord. And because of these abominations the Lord your God is driving them out before you. You shall be blameless before the Lord your God, for these nations, which you are about to dispossess, listen to fortune-tellers and to diviners. But as for you, the Lord your God has not allowed you to do this."* (Deut. 18:9-14)

I spoke to one of the senior crewmen and asked him what there was about the latent power of the soul that made this ship so attractive? He told me how God in the beginning places His spirit into man and said, *"man became a living soul"* That part of the man that is of God is his spirit, and that which is of the flesh is his soul. Man is created tripartite; body, soul, and spirit. (1 Thess. 5:23) The Spirit gives God consciousness, the soul produces self-consciousness, and the body produces world consciousness.

God told Adam to *be fruitful and multiply, fill the earth and subdue it; have dominion over the fish of the sea, over the birds of the air, and over every living thing that moves on the earth.* These words in Hebrew mean that Adam was to be God's Kingdom agent and he was to rule and subdue all creation, including the satanic forces present on earth. (Genesis 1:28)

God gave Adam a Herculean task when he asked him to name every living creature. There are certain creatures that are unique to each continent. There are kangaroos that live only in Australia and giraffes that only live in Africa. There's the North American moose and the Asian panda to name a few of these animals found only in certain areas of the world. The task of naming all the animals would require Adam to travel all over the world. The intellectual ability to name hundreds and thousands of species of insects and birds and other animals is unbelievable, even in this modern computer age. Some believe that Adam used astral travel to move around the world. This is the same spiritual power that moved Philip in the 8th chapter of the Book of Acts, from a desert place where he was speaking with the Ethiopian eunuch to Azotus in Samaria. *"The spirit of the Lord caught Philip away."* Many Eastern mystics meditating on their "magic carpets" had been suddenly transported from one area of the world to another.

Adam was placed in charge of the Garden of Eden and told to dress it and keep it. We can assume the garden was quite large since four different rivers flowed out from the garden. Adam, before the fall, was a superhuman. He was created in the image of God!

There were two sacred trees in the midst of the garden, the tree of life, and the tree of the knowledge of good and evil. Adam and Eve were told not to eat of it or touch either tree, less they die. There was the serpent in the garden that spoke to Eve from the tree of the knowledge of good and evil and told her."

> *"She would not surely die for God knows that your eyes will be opened, and you will be like God knowing good and evil." When "the woman saw that the tree was good for food, that was pleasant to the eyes, and a tree desirable to make one wise, she took up its fruit and ate. She also gave it to her husband with her and he ate." (Gen. 3:4-6)*

Satan has always coveted the latent power available in the soul of man. When Adam fell his soul was damaged because of his sin. Adam was created to rule the earth, a Co-Regent with God or a Prince. When Adam fell Satan became the *"Prince of this world"* and Adam forfeited his rule because of his sin. The power of the soul was hidden in Adam's flesh but never lost. Some of that latent power in man's soul can be restored through various occult practices of asceticism, fasting, and meditation. The ancient Babylonians, Arab mystics, Buddhist, Taoists, and Hindus all have developed techniques to release the hidden power of the soul. They learned that the flesh could be displaced by fasting from food, sex, and heavy physical exercise as well as repetitive prayer using prayer beads, and by performing certain aesthetic practices and hardships, such as self-inflicted pain like lying on a bed of nails. Their meditation technique requires them to empty their mind and often say repetitive prayers to demonic deities. Christians need to be warned never to empty their minds when meditating on our Lord and avoid passivity. Drugs, hypnotism, and alcohol can produce a passive state of the mind, which allows demonic intrusion. ***Christian meditation is supposed to be active, never passive.*** It's to be focused on our Lord. Passive meditation allows demonic spirits to enter a man's soul. Unfortunately, many Christian leaders encourage people to be involved in meditation practices that produce a passivity of the mind and the entrance of deception and demonic thoughts.

God never works through a man's soul power. God works through the Holy Spirit. God hates the use of the power of the soul. It is an anathema to God and forbidden of men. We are to crucify our soul life and find a new life through the Spirit in Christ.

Satan's plan is to use man's soulishness as his instrument to resist God. Demonic powers may influence men to produce false repentance, false salvation, false revival, false peace, false joy, and false works of the Holy Spirit including miracles and wonders, which are counterfeits of the workings of the Holy Spirit. We are to resist and bind that which comes out of the self-life and be submitted to the power of the Holy Spirit. We are all vulnerable to not trusting in the power of the Holy Spirit and to use our own flesh, psychological power, and soul power to manipulate people. Submission to the Spirit of God means to refuse to exert any power of the flesh against the spirit of God. It is often tempting to try and help God using soulish methods. God doesn't need or want any help from our flesh. We cannot manipulate God by shouting, weeping, jumping, incessant singing of choruses, videos, power point presentations, testimonies, or other types of moving stories. God, under the inspiration of the Holy Spirit may use music, dramatic testimonies, videos, and a variety of contemporary techniques for His purposes. The issue is always the question: "Is this a work of the Holy Spirit, a work of man, or even a work of demons?"

We must remember that the only thing that can return to a Holy God is something that came from God in the first place. Only those works by the Holy Spirit in cooperation with our spirit can be pleasing to God. Our power comes through submission to the Spirit of God. In the Book of John, the Lord says, "*it is the spirit that gives life; the flesh profits nothing,*" (John 6:63). Even Jesus said: "*the Son can do nothing of himself, but what he sees the father doing,*" (John 5:19). Only the Spirit of God can bring life to others.

Sorcery is defined as divination with the help of the demonic spirits. There was a certain slave girl in Acts 16 possessed with a spirit of divination who followed Paul and correctly called Paul and associates *"servants of the Most High God."* Many Christians would call this woman in Acts 16 a prophet because her prophetic statement was correct and edifying. Supernatural acts are just that; acts that come from the spirit world. Christians must discern whether this word or action is from the dark side or from the light side of the spirit world by the Holy Spirit. Authenticity, accuracy, and something seemingly very supernatural is no guarantee that an act or word comes from God. Satan will bring strong delusion in these days. According to 2 Thessalonians 2:9-12, God tells us:

> *"The coming of the lawless one is by the activity of Satan with all power and false signs and wonders, and with all wicked deception for those who are perishing, because they refused to love the truth and so be saved. Therefore, God sends them a strong delusion, so that they may believe what is false, in order that all may be condemned who did not believe the truth but had pleasure in unrighteousness."*

It is the love of the truth that brings discernment and protection from deception. Christians unknowingly may practice "Christian Witchcraft." By which I mean praying aggressively and relentlessly for something to happen which is against the will of God. Witchcraft occurs when we call on power from non-Christian sources to have our will rather than His will. Whenever we choose to make God respond to our desires or pray against His will, we are using the latent power of our souls, and indirectly demonic power, to have our own way. We are attempting to use God as our servant! Well-meaning Christians are frequently asked to pray for others. They respond with compassion and pray without asking God for direction on how to pray assuming that they know God's will! Unknowingly, they may be praying against God's will. When we pray against God's will we are binding the work of the Holy Spirit. Jesus taught the disciples to pray as follows:

> *"Pray then like this: "Our Father in heaven, hallowed be your name. Your kingdom come, **your will be done, on earth as it is in heaven**." (Matt. 6:9-10)*

Be careful how you pray. *"Truly, I say to you, whatever you bind on earth shall be bound in heaven, and whatever you loose on earth shall be loosed in heaven."* (Matt. 18:18)

Always ask God for direction before praying. Prayer is meant to be two-way communication with God. Our prayers must begin with *thy will be done; thy kingdom come.* We are arrogant and dangerous when we think we know God's will and act without asking Him! Only that which comes from the Father can please the Father. Prayer begins with the question; "Father what are you doing and what do you want me to do?"

Jesus sets the example for us in John 5:19: "" *The Son can do nothing of himself, but what he sees the Father do."* The word for "sees" (*blepo* in Greek) signifies to contemplate, to perceive, to know. Later in chapter 5 verse 30 Jesus says: *"I can do nothing on my own. As I hear, I judge, and my judgment is just, because I seek not my own will but the will of him who sent me."*

John 7:18 Jesus says: *"The one who speaks on his own authority seeks his own glory; but the one who seeks the glory of Him who sent Him is true, and in Him there is no falsehood."*

If we abide in Him and seek His will, we will bear much fruit. John 15:4: *"Abide in me, and I in you. As the branch cannot bear fruit by itself, unless it abides in the vine, neither can you, unless you abide in me."*

The Holy Spirit will tell us of the Father's will, so we know how to pray. John 16:13-15 says, *"When the Spirit of truth comes, He will guide you into all the truth, for He will not speak on His own authority, but whatever He hears He will speak, and He will declare to you the things that are to come. He will glorify Me, for He will take what is Mine and declare it to you. All that the Father has is Mine; therefore, I said that He will take what is mine and declare it to you."*

Christians are very naive about the dangers of various occultic practices because they are often disguised as being very spiritual. Satan's desire is to bring confusion and deception into God's church. The deeper things of the spirit are not generally taught in Christian circles. This makes Christians very vulnerable to deception. Satan's greatest deception is to minimize and hide the demonic work in the soul of man! Christians don't think that they are vulnerable to demonic deception and therefore ignore it. Satan works behind the scenes to bring confusion and deception to Christians and eventually enslave them to do his will just as he did to Eve.

> *"But I am afraid that as the serpent deceived Eve by his cunning, your thoughts will be led astray from a sincere and pure devotion to Christ. For if someone comes and proclaims another Jesus than the one, we proclaimed, or if you receive a different spirit from the one you received, or if you accept a different gospel from the one you accepted, you put up with it readily enough."* (2 Cor. 11:3-4)

We live in a day where mystical spirituality has become increasingly common. Instead of fear of mixing light and darkness, many church leaders are embracing Eastern, particularly Buddhist and Hindu meditation practices to their peril. This is called "contemplative or centering prayer." New age techniques such as chanting, guided imagery, prayer beads, repetitive singing, body discipline such as yoga, breathing techniques, and others are used for channeling into the mystical realm of the supernatural. Aesthetic practice such as vegetarianism, fasting, and abstaining from marriage and sexual relations are encouraged. The hope is to find the "true self" or "divine center." Paul warned Timothy about these practices in chapter 4:1-4 of his first letter to Timothy.

> *"Now the Spirit expressly says that in later times some will depart from the faith by devoting them-*

selves to deceitful spirits and teachings of demons, through the insincerity of liars whose consciences are seared, who forbid marriage and require abstinence from foods that God created to be received with thanksgiving by those who believe and know the truth. For everything created by God is good, and nothing is to be rejected if it is received with thanksgiving, for it is made holy by the word of God and prayer."

The center of man is the self and Jesus came to slay the self since the self is always in opposition to God. *"For out of the heart come evil thoughts, murder, adultery, sexual immorality, theft, false witness, slander."* (Matt. 15:19) A true Christian is God-centered and not self-centered. The "New Christianity" is about replacing God on His throne with man. The sarcastic French atheist Voltaire once commented that "If God has made us in His Image, we have returned the favor!"

The *Deception*, the dragon ship, seemed to snake its way between the other ships using its long tail for propulsion and many people left their ships to find power and identity there so that they too would be like Eve and "be like God!" The crewman assured me that according to Isaiah, eventually the Sword of the Lord would destroy the twisted serpent or dragon ship in God's perfect time.

"O Lord, how manifold are your works! In wisdom have you made them all; the earth is full of your creatures. Here is the sea, great and wide, which teems with creatures innumerable, living things both small and great. There go the ships, and Leviathan, which you formed to play in it." (Ps. 104:24-26)

"In that day the Lord with his hard and great and strong sword will punish Leviathan the fleeing serpent, Leviathan the twisting serpent, and he will slay the dragon that is in the sea." (Isa. 27:1)

Chapter 17

KINGDOM LIVING

I thought of the words of the Master Mariner. He never said that he came to establish a church with man as the center but to establish the Kingdom of God. The Kingdom of God is where the King lives, rules, and reigns. Those who are in the Kingdom are to be about the King's business. Religion is about man's attempt to find God based on his own efforts. The Kingdom of God is about the King and not about men. Men are admitted into the Kingdom of God at the King's choosing. Many who enter the Kingdom of God will fall away. Kingdom life is about our relationship with our Lord and not religious works. Kingdom living and religion seem so close, yet they are so far apart. We forget that there is nothing tainted by man's work that can endure in the Kingdom. It's all about the King's work through man's hands and the transformation of man by the Spirit of God.

If man could help himself then he would share in God's glory. But since man can't help himself and is lost, he cannot contribute or take anything from God's glory. The King demands the Lordship of all we are and all we own. Where the King is, he rules, and there's no compromise. He demands to be King now and not later. If he's not King now in our life he's not going to be King later. If we know the Kingdom now, we know something of heaven. Again, if we don't see something of heaven now, we will not see it in the future. Many are looking for their future in Paradise and want to delay the Lordship of the King to the very last minute. They think they can avoid Lordship yet make it into paradise. Unfortunately, he's King now or never. Paradise is the benefit of Kingdom living. If we do not live for the King now, we cannot fellowship with the King later! You may ask, how can the Kingdom of God be now, when there is suffering, and persecution and trials and we live in a wicked world? Isn't the Kingdom of God about freedom from suffering in trials, and you say it's heaven now and the question of course is how can that be? Heaven is about worshiping, obeying, and fellowshipping with our King. Heavenly worship transcends the troubles of this world. We also know that the Kingdom of God is at war with the kingdoms, powers and principalities of the underworld. The Kingdom of God will always be under assault until that day when all the Lord's enemies are vanquished. The joy of the Lord is about standing with the King at our side as we do battle with the enemies of the King. When we feel the presence of the King, suffering seems to be of no concern. To be standing shoulder to shoulder with the King and our fellow Saints is all that matters. This is a little of heaven now because the King has told us we will rule and reign with Him which begins now on earth. To understand we must stand with Him now clothed in the armor of God doing battle with his enemies. The Kingdom of God is not completely understood, yet it is to be experienced by all believers.

The Promised Land is a type and shadow of the Kingdom of God. It is the place of testing where we work out our salvation with fear and trembling. The Israelites left the desert, a type of the secular world or sea of humanity, and crossed the Jordan River, a type of baptism, into the Promised Land. The Promised Land is a place of battles, trials, and often suffering and is a type or shadow of the Kingdom of God. It is not a place of rest!

Suddenly, I saw a great ship that glowed in the twilight. It was named *"Salvation through Baptism."* It had a large swimming pool on the top deck. The pool was very deep. Those who jumped into the pool were submerged by the water and when they came up for air they claimed that they had entered the Kingdom of God after being submerged and having a neardeath

experience. Baptism speaks of death to the old man, a voluntary laying down of one's life by drowning, and resurrection into a new life in Christ. This is the work of God's spirit in the sincere believer. Baptism cannot of itself save anyone yet is required of all believers when possible. It seals a covenantal transaction between man and God. It is a visible sign to the spirit world that this new creation in Christ now belongs to God! As I observed this, I asked the mate if it was only through water and the spirit that we entered the kingdom. No, he said, we also enter through the baptism of fire and repentance. Many enter during a time of difficult trials.

I noted many people who claimed a relationship with our Lord but produced little or no fruit for the Kingdom. The crew explained to me that our Lord had written in His Chart Book that there would always be mixture. At the end of time, he will separate the wheat from the tares. The tares would be burnt with fire, but that wheat would be harvested and then stored in His barns. I pondered how a holy God could allow any mixture in His kingdom. The crew reminded me that God is merciful. Judas was one of the twelve and enjoyed intimate fellowship with our Lord. God has his purposes for allowing tares to grow with the wheat. The tares, they explained, are like those with a superficial relationship with the Lord based on head knowledge rather than heart knowledge. They look like wheat and cannot be detected until full grown when there is no fruit.

Men comfort themselves in what they believe in the Chart Book of God. They confuse intellectual understanding and acceptance with saving faith. It is heart knowledge that results in transformation. God places in a man's heart true faith. It is a work of God and not man. A change in mind or intellectual acceptance does not produce a changed heart. It is a changed heart that produces a changed mind. Thus, God works through the heart to reach the head. Head down Christianity or trickle-down Christianity, from the head or intellect, rarely produces true heart knowledge.

Men with heart knowledge are not moved by threats of torture, cruelty, or even death. Men with head knowledge are fearful of men and can be persuaded to reject God and change their minds. The double minded man is unstable in all his ways. Why? Because he thinks he can be saved by what he believes rather than whom he knows personally, i.e., Jesus. It is better to hope in who you know and His character and promises rather than a mind trip and works of righteousness. The Chart Book reminds us that we are not saved by works of righteousness but according to God's mercy and grace. He saved us through the washing, regeneration, and renewing of the Holy Spirit. All the glory goes to God and none to man. If man contributes anything to his salvation, then he steals glory from God and God will not share his glory with any other!

The nature of the Kingdom of God is that there is always a battle for the center. Man is always striving to push God out of the way and be the center of the Kingdom. This is illustrated in the doctrine of the Nicolaitans spoken in the Chart Book in Revelation 2 verses 6 and 15. The word Nicolaitans is derived from two Greek words *nicos* and *laos*. *Nicos* means to conquer or overcome, and we get the word Nike from the same root Greek word. *Laos* is the Greek root word for people or laity. Nicolaitans means to conquer the laity. This speaks of the division of the church into a high priestly cast or clergy based on superior knowledge and gifting. Our Lord tells us that He hates the doctrine of the Nicolaitans. The Chart Book tells us that all men are kings and priests. There is no special priestly caste. There's only one high priest, Master Mariner, and Lord.

> *"As you come to him, a living stone rejected by men but in the sight of God chosen and precious, ^{you} yourselves like living stones are being built up as a spiritual house, to be a <u>holy priesthood,</u> to offer spiritual sacrifices acceptable to God through Jesus Christ." (1 Peter 2:4-5)*
>
> *"But you are a chosen generation, <u>a royal priesthood,</u> a holy nation, His own special people, that you may proclaim the praises of Him who called you out of darkness into His marvelous*

light;" (1 Peter 2:9) The word in Greek for royal
is *basilikos* (βασιλικός), "belonging to a king,""

Every Christian is called to function in his Royal Priesthood and to exercise this function daily in his home and work sustained by the power of the Holy Spirit. He is to be a light and agent of change in the secular business world. This does not happen very effectively unless those in the ministering priesthood nourish, encourage, guide, and sustain the saints. The church cannot function without servant leadership.

The division of the church into clergy and laypeople was never modeled in the early church. The apostles call themselves *doulos*, which in Greek means bondservants! The biblical model is for servant leaders who don't lord it over people based on their own abilities and personal holiness. God's plan is for holy men to lead by gifting and anointing rather than by office. The carnal man wants to lead and control by office or position rather than gifting and anointing. Unfortunately, power and elitism usually leads to sin. God's plan is that we be submitted humbly one to another. There are many Christians who have been hurt by church leaders. However, anticlericalism is just as poisonous as clericalism. We are all guilty of putting too much hope in the institutional church, which will bring disappointment. The church is not the hope of history but God's instrument for the perfecting of the bride who is God's eternal purpose and plan. The Bride of Christ includes all the saints inside and outside of the church or the community of all believers' dead and alive.

Unfortunately, the Western model of pastoring is teaching truth rather than modeling truth. Somehow, we think we can teach and train others in what we ourselves don't live! It always seemed to me so ironic, as I once picketed abortion clinics as a prolife physician, that I walked with Catholic priests but never picketed with or was shoulder to shoulder with a protestant evangelical leader once in my many fights over pro-life issues. Protestant pastors tell people what to do from the rear and safety of the pulpit, but usully do not lead from the front setting the example for others to follow! Jesus led from the front and overturned the tables of the moneychangers! Many church leaders have lost credibility by living lifestyles that do not model the values and socio-economic conditions of their flock.

The role of the average church pastor is very distorted indeed. He is expected to be a good teacher within certain limits and avoid subjects that are too controversial. He is expected to visit the sick as well as council and shepherd the flock and be a good evangelist. Meanwhile the pew-sitter has no expectation for himself, other than financially support the pastor who is supposed to do all the work of the ministry! How twisted, but this is the average American church! This is just the opposite of what is biblical. The biblical role of leadership is to lead by example and train and help others operate in their gifting, thus enabling the saints to do the work of the ministry. Many wonder, how can you run a ship without a chief leader or Captain? True servant leaders lead from the front by their gifting, anointing, and abilities. Most of all they model what they preach, through which they equip and train others to run the ship. (Ephesians 4:11-12) A great leader is seen by the work and example of his disciples even though he is not visible, yet still leading by his spirit.

> *"The kings of the Gentiles exercise lordship over them, and those in authority over them are called benefactors. But not so with you. Rather, let the greatest among you become as the youngest, and the leader as one who serves. For whom is the greater, one who reclines at table or one who serves? Is it not the one who reclines at table? But I am among you as the one who serves."* (Luke 22:25-27)

> Jesus said: *"But I am among you as the one who serves,"* (Luke 22:27).

Servant leaders must be humble and realize that they can do nothing by themselves.

"My teaching is not mine, but his who sent me."
(John 7:16)

*"I do nothing on my own authority but speak just
as the Father taught me." (John 8:28)*

"Yet I do not seek my own glory." (John 8:50)

*"So Jesus said to them, "Truly, truly, I say to you,
the Son can do nothing of his own accord, but
only what he sees the Father doing. For whatever
the Father does, that the Son does likewise." (John
5:19)*

*"I can do nothing on my own. As I hear, I judge,
and my judgment is just, because I seek not my
own will but the will of him who sent me." (John
5:30)*

*"The words that I say to you I do not speak on
my own authority, but the Father who dwells in me
does his works." (John 14:10)*

The mature leader lets God lead and work through him and
makes no attempt to do anything on his own volition. It is God's
work, and He will do it if we get out of His way!

Perhaps the most important quality for leadership is broken-
ness. Men desire to be filled with the Holy Spirit but cannot be
filled unless they are empty! We must understand that we have
nothing and are nothing. God doesn't need us but chooses to use us
for His own mysterious reasons!

*"But we have this treasure in jars of clay, to show
that the surpassing power belongs to God and
not to us." (2 Cor. 4:7) ... "For we who live are
always being given over to death for Jesus' sake,
so that the life of Jesus also may be manifested in*

our mortal flesh. So death is at work in us, but life in you." (2 Cor. 4:11-12)

We are nothing but very ordinary clay pots. Furthermore, we are "Cracked pots" who leak and need constant refreshing and refilling at the fountain of God. We are just ordinary clay in the master potter's hands who shapes us into useful vessels for His purpose without consulting us! It is not for us to know why but simply obey.

> *"Shall the potter be regarded as the clay, that the thing made should say of its maker, "He did not make me"; or the thing formed say of him who formed it, "He has no understanding"? (Isa. 29:16)*

Pottery is fragile and easily broken. This is again according to God's purpose. When the outer shell is broken then the light within can shine out to a lost world. Death to us brings life to others.

Under proper Spirit led servant leadership the ship runs smoothly because each man is given responsibility in the area of his gifting and ability. There is harmony on the ship when each crewman has identified his gift and is functioning in that gift. When all are pulling together the ship moves forward because there is no division or competition. There's no jealousy, slander, or back-biting in such a ship. Competition and division occur when people are jockeying for position. Our Master Mariner told us that the servant is not greater than his Master and he who is servant is the greatest of all. The Captain was a gray-haired servant leader who distained titles and was respected by all for his knowledge of the Chart Book and his ability to be guided by the Master Mariner. His ears had grown very large over the years as he learned to hear the quiet small voice of his Master. He was always approachable, humble, and led by example. He never asked the crew to do anything that he wouldn't also do.

"But whoever would be great among you must be your servant, and whoever would be first among you must be slave of all. For even the Son of Man came not to be served but to serve, and to give his life as a ransom for many." (Mark 10:43-45)

If a man hasn't learned to serve quietly, faithfully, and without notice, he is not ready for leadership. The authority pattern in Scripture is that the apostles appointed elders in every city. These were generally gray haired older experienced working family men with one current wife and blameless children. He had to have a proven credibility and service in the community.

> *"He must not be a recent convert, or he may become puffed up with conceit and fall into the condemnation of the devil. Moreover, he must be well thought of by outsiders, so that he may not fall into disgrace, into a snare of the devil."* (1 Tim. 3:6-7)

Jewish tradition was that a man was under his father's tutelage from age twelve until age thirty. This is why Jesus didn't begin His ministry until after age thirty. There is no support for the beginning of church ministry in the early twenties without life and work experiences. Paul was a tentmaker who chose to set the example for others by supporting himself by his trade even though he could have rightly asked to be supported by the church in Jerusalem. Instead, he raised funds for the Jerusalem church. Paul, who had already earned the equivalent of a Doctor of Theology in Jerusalem before his conversion, went to Arabia after his conversion and three years later went up to Jerusalem to see Peter. He then went into Syria and Cilicia for fourteen years before returning to Jerusalem with Barnabas. Brilliant Paul needed a desert experience with God before he was ready for ministry. (Gal. 1:17-2:1) Paul was also a tentmaker who could be self-supporting when necessary. (1 Cor. 9:12)

Paul was no inexperienced youth or flash in the pan, but a mature man humbled and disciplined by God who was not arrogant or greedy for gain. He had died to self and had no one to please except God!

> *"He must not be arrogant or quick-tempered or a drunkard or violent or greedy for gain, but hospitable, a lover of good, self-controlled, upright, holy, and disciplined. He must hold firm to the trustworthy word as taught, so that he may be able to give instruction in sound doctrine and also to rebuke those who contradict it."* (Tit. 1:7-9)

Too many leaders today are greedy for gain and do not give instruction in sound doctrine for fear of offending men. Many are lazy and expect others to do the hard work. Too often many distain theology and offer vacuous platitudes and avoid talking about sin and the eternal damnation of the unrepentant sinner.

Small ships require all men to work. Men are cross trained to do each other's job. We understand that men naturally are lazy, prideful, and selfish. Our old ship required all men to work, and they worked hard, knowing they were about the business of the Master Mariner. A properly working ship places men in a position requiring them to depend on each other and honor each others' gifts or the ship will sink. The men on our ship loved each other and demonstrated that by their unselfishness, praise, and appreciation for one another. They were willing to lay their lives down for one another.

This type of servant leadership works well in small ships such as ours, because there is accountability and transparency amongst the crewmen. In larger ships there are people who want the benefit of the group but not the responsibility of service. They may try to join a congregation in order to obtain power. Carnal leaders want the true humble spiritual leaders to do all the work of the ministry such as visiting the sick, helping the poor, and counseling the needy. This frees them from responsibility and enables them to live the lie. These are false leaders who think they can hide behind position and avoid the work of the ministry. These types of carnal leaders trusted and manipulated men to keep them in their position rather than trusting God. They had become in bondage to the opinions of men and offered easy grace, and preached Christ without the cross.

These are men who teach easy believism and cheap grace which allows men to think they can escape the damnation of God by what they believe rather than what they live. Cheap grace offers men a cheap ticket to heaven that provides them an eternal life in a beautiful paradise from a travel brochure. This at little cost or no cost if you get a special on a certain unnamed television network! Their dogs and animals will go to heaven with those who "accept Jesus." They will see all their friends and relatives and probably find a beautiful golf course. They will have eternal joy and eternal security and party, party, party. There's more emphasis on the benefits of heaven than the benefactor!

Costly grace is about having more of our Lord and less of ourselves in Heaven. When we get into the presence of our glorified Lord, He will so fill our minds and souls with His Glory that there will be little room to think of anything else but to worship Him. He will become greater and greater, and we will become smaller and smaller as we understand his marvelous mercy and grace. True Heaven is all about Him and His Glory and not about us. A false, cheap gospel produces scattered and sick sheep if it produces any sheep at all.

> "Woe to the shepherds who destroy and scatter the sheep of my pasture!" declares the Lord. Therefore, thus says the Lord, the God of Israel, concerning the shepherds who care for my people: "You have scattered my flock and have driven them away, and you have not attended to them. Behold, I will attend to you for your evil deeds, declares the Lord. Then I will gather the remnant of my flock out of all the countries where I have driven them, and I will bring them back to their fold, and they shall be fruitful and multiply. I will

*set shepherds over them who will care for them,
and they shall fear no more, nor be dismayed,
neither shall any be missing, declares the Lord."*
(Jer. 23:1-4)

As we got closer to our destination, the sea around us became increasingly crowded with thousands of ships. Some were large ships, and some were small ships. Many people jumped from one ship to another. It appeared that there were more people jumping from smaller ships to bigger ships because they had more attractive programs. The larger ships had all kinds of advertising on the sides of the hulls such as "userfriendly, great children's programs, Starbucks coffee here." In the midst of the ships were teaching ships or conference ships that focused on how to attract people to your ship. The userfriendly ships promised position, power, prosperity, and glorified man. They worshiped a different savior than we did. These men felt that if they had said the sinners' prayer, then God was obligated to save them! Obedience was conditional to these carnal men, and only when it was convenient, or someone was watching! Their savior did not deliver them from the love of this world and its powers. Yet they still expected to find eternal life. It always seems so strange to me that people could expect the blessings from their relationship with our risen Lord without paying a significant price. Their teachers often taught that the master had been nailed to the mast and paid the price for their sins. Since the price of redemption was paid, salvation was a free gift! I wondered, if people, deep down in their hearts, didn't recognize that the priceless sacrifice of our Savior was of such immensity that it demanded the same type of sacrifice from us. They like to hear that the gift was paid, and they were free to do their own thing. However, the message of the costly gifts doesn't sell well in a multicultural society where men live for themselves.

A costly gift is valued because it's an inestimable price. Cheap gifts are not valued for long and eventually trodden underfoot. It was tragic to see that this cheap grace was being sold in the marketplace of ships to exploit confused man. So often a lie sells better than the truth, particularly, when the truth would cost you everything. Some of these ship leaders would say almost anything to bring the sheep into the ship. These men are really wolves in sheep's clothing because they lie to the sheep and deceive them, so they never find their true shepherd. These false shepherds fear other men more than they fear God. They cast spells and create illusions for man by bringing half-truths. They give false comfort to those that are damned. They are the men that manipulate and deceive the damned.

The Master Mariner has said in his Chart Book that He is against these false shepherds and will require His flock at their hand. He will seek the sheep and deliver them from all places where they have been scattered. He will judge between rams and goats and will also judge between the fat and lean sheep. It is so comforting to know that His flock will no longer be used as prey for false shepherds and the sheep will be free to worship the true shepherd. Our Lord tells us that He did not send these prophets, yet they ran and He had not spoken to them, yet they prophesied. But if they had stood in His counsel and had caused His people to hear His words then they would have turned from the evil way and from the evil of their doings. He is against these prophets who use their tongues and say that "He says" He is against those who prophesy false dreams and cause His people to err by their lies and their recklessness. They perverted the words of the living God and God promises an everlasting reproach on them!

The third commandment is that "*You shall not take the Lord's name in vain, for the Lord will not hold him guiltless who takes His name in vain.*" Many people ignore their real issue in this commandment and simply think it means abstaining from swear words. The real issue is to say, "God says" and misrepresent God's word and character not only by words but by actions! We feel so spiritual when we say God told me such and such. Often the words "God has revealed to me" or "God told me to tell you"Etc. are a powerful way to manipulate people. It is an easy way to end an argument by saying, "Well God told me that your view is wrong!" It is better to say, "Could God be speaking about...etc.?" or "I hear God very imperfectly, but I think God is saying... What do you think?" It is painful to our Lord to hear His name used time and time again when He has not spoken! Be careful! Remember do not take the Lord's Name in vain. Deuteronomy 18:20 warns us:

> "But the prophet who presumes to speak a word in my name that I have not commanded him to speak, or who speaks in the name of other gods, that same prophet shall die."

True believers know that the present afflictions of this world are transient and small compared of the glorious future and eternal reward that those who love the Lord will receive. We believers are *sorrowful but always rejoicing, as poor yet making many rich, as having nothing but possessing all things* (2 Cor. 6:10). We know that we are aliens, pilgrims, or sojourners in this present world and our citizenship is in heaven and not on earth. (1 Pet. 2:11; Heb. 11:13) The unsaved in this world are clinging to every worldly sensual experience that they can during their short lifetime. Believers know they're passing through a foreign land where they don't belong. They understand that in retrospect the transit time on this earth will be insignificant when compared to an eternity with our Lord and Savior. The things of this world have little attraction to them if they keep their eyes on the Master Mariner. They can see both this world, which is under judgment and will be destroyed, and the New World to come. Believers understand that the promises of this world can never satisfy. They mourn for those who trust in idols that will never satisfy. Their hope is in things eternal.

Chapters 18

HOPE IN JESUS

I was feeling very comfortable on my ship, the 3Ts, and this old rust bucket became increasingly more beautiful in my eyes. I felt peace and safety and developed increasing boldness, no longer fearing man or death. I just looked forward to meeting my Savior. I had the assurance that no matter what difficulties lay ahead, somehow, we would make it to the Promised Land. I was getting restless, so I was given a job that suited my gifting. I was asked to be a life ring thrower. I was given a large pile of life rings, each with a rope that was attached to the ship. I stationed myself from the stern of the ship on a platform close to the water. This was the ideal place where I could throw the life rings to those who cried out for mercy and were afraid of drowning. I saw life rings floating in the sea that had blinking lights and promised salvation to those who would grab hold of them. They were the carefully crafted works of men that promised salvation by works but actually brought death to those that rested on them. Those life rings were much more attractive than ours. They were shiny and bejeweled and had many small lights. There was even a little loudspeaker on each life ring that made great promises to men. Our life rings were dirty, bruised, beaten, bloody, and comparably unattractive. Yet these life rings possessed the power of life to those that rested on them. It was interesting to note that all the life rings, even those that promised false hope, had painted on them "Word of God." The mate told me that it's only the anointed Word of God that saves men and it's the message of sacrifice and turning away from all in this life that brings some to life; those that grasp the true word of God. Once the cost is understood many others will fall away. The mystery is we gain our life by losing it.

> Jesus said in Mark 8:35, "*If anyone would come after me, let him deny himself and take up his cross and follow me. For whoever would save his life will lose it, but whoever loses his life for my sake and the gospel's will save it.*"

I asked the mate to help me discern among all the people floating in the sea who would be willing candidates for our life rings. He told me to select those that had *big ears*. "Big ears," I said, "why?" He told me that only those with big ears could hear about the regenerating power of the Holy Spirit and would grasp the anointed life rings with both hands and never let go. The Holy Spirit goes before and touches or regenerates men called of God, so that in time they might hear and obey the gospel and be converted. He gives them ears to hear. For Isaiah says, "*Lord, who has believed what he has heard from us?*" So, faith comes from hearing, and hearing through the word of Christ, (Rom. 10:17). God is the one who opens ears so men might hear and by faith be saved. The life rings must be grasped with both hands, holding on with both faith and repentance if one is to be saved. When the word of God has done its regenerative work, it produces not only faith but repentance or a turning around from focus on the self and the world to focus on God and acts of righteousness that please God.

The word obey in the Greek is *hupakouo* and is translated to "hear under" or hearing or listening with the intent and purpose of obeying, to harken, to be subject to, to heed, to conform, to make a religious decision. How many times have we heard our disobedient children claim that they disobeyed because they didn't hear us? Obedience is conditional on purposeful hearing of God's word. "***This is my beloved Son; <u>listen to him</u>.***" (Mark 9:7)

"And being made perfect, **he became the source of eternal salvation to all who obey** (hearing with the purpose of obeying) **him.**" (Heb. 5:9)

> Jesus determines those who will hear. He told His disciples: *"This is why I speak to them in parables, because seeing they do not see, and hearing they do not hear, nor do they understand. Indeed, in their case the prophecy of Isaiah is fulfilled that says: "'You will indeed hear but never understand, and you will indeed see but never perceive. For this people's heart has grown dull, and with their ears they can barely hear, and their eyes they have closed, lest they should see with their eyes and hear with their ears and understand with their heart and turn, and I would heal them.' But blessed are your eyes, for they see, and your ears, for they hear."* (Matt. 13:13-15)

The life rings were attached to a rope that was attached to the ship so we could pull those with big ears and who were attached to the life rings on board. I asked the mate about the rope attached to the life ring and he said that the rope was made out of the prayers of the saints.

Many others in the sea were rather indifferent to our ship and even though life rings were always offered, they mocked us and stated they were looking for something much better than this old rusting hulk. The mate had warned me to be careful with our life rings and not to waste our precious supply on those who did not desire to come aboard our ship. Once the supply of the life rings was exhausted all the survivors and crew were brought aboard; the stern platform was raised and the door to the ship was closed in preparation for the storms ahead.

Aboard the ship there was lots of activity and very useful levels of authority. Those in leadership wore servants' clothing and aprons. The leaders had washed the feet of all the passengers and other crewmen. Each person was prayed for to find their spiritual gifting and then placed in the appropriate position on the ship. Every passenger found his place and became part of the crew, so really there were no more passengers, just crewmen aboard the ship.

The vision of the captain and the crew was to get the ship through the storms, rocky shoals, whirlpools, and other dangers to the shore of the Promised Land. Some of the crew would disembark at that point and continue their walk. Other crewmen would stay with the captain who would take the ship back out to sea to pick up more passengers. The second mate testified that it was the Holy Spirit who filled the sails and brought power to the ship. He also claimed that it was the Holy Spirit who was the navigator and guided the captain through the Chart Book, the Book of Life. Various Scripture passages warned the crew of dangers and shipwrecks along the way. It also warned of the trials to come. It was the Word of God, which guided us and showed us the secret way through coral reefs and rocky places. The ship was unique in that it was strong but flexible.

The crew told us the story of the Master Mariner who lived a perfect life and was born by a virgin but rejected by men. Angry men nailed him to the yardarm, and he was pulled up along the mast, so he became a spectacle for the whole world to see. He died and was sent to the bottom of the sea and arose to sit on the right hand of the Creator of all things. He promised to return for his shipmates and then bring them aboard his ship of eternal glory. It was the hope of seeing the Savior that brought excitement and energy to the ship. There were several shipmates who had hoped the Master Mariner was coming soon and would take them out of the ship and directly to heaven, thus avoiding tribulation and suffering. The captain comforted us with the words of the Master Mariner who said that of those who love him, none would be lost. There would be difficulties ahead, but he knew that no one on the ship would be lost. This brought great joy to the crew. It took the fear away from many who were afraid of the troubles ahead and now they could rejoice knowing that no difficulty, trial, or tribulation could ever separate them from the loving arms of the Master Mariner. (John 6:39, 10:29, 17:12)

We looked around at the other ships, which were listless, and seemingly without power. The sailing ships had no wind and the engine-powered ships seemed to have no power. That is because they were powered by man's ingenuity, cleverness, and works rather than by the guidance and wind of the Holy Spirit. One of the crewmen said to me that man cannot make it to the Promised Land based on his own efforts and cleverness. It seemed the tables had turned. We had the wind of the spirit filling our sails. Those mighty ships that had earlier mocked our poor dilapidated ship and sped by us in demonstrations of their great power now were jealous of the blessing of God that was upon us. They had laughed at us and seemed to try and come close to us to swamp us in their wake. The captains of the ships mocked our navigator since he chose a different route which seemed much more difficult and dangerous. The other ship navigators claimed that our Chart Book was old and out of date and we needed a more modern translation to guide us with updated charts, notes, and a concordance. They didn't understand that the Master Mariner had promised to teach those that fear Him, his secrets. God promises to those who love Him, to bring them through uncharted waters to safety. He promised that He would guide and teach the humble. Most of the ships chose the easy way to try and avoid any difficulties. The other ships seemed to hold back and were watching where we were going since they didn't have clear guidance. Some decided to follow us.

Chapter 19

Trials and Troubles

God's plan for their lives. When we look at the cost of losing all to gain the Master Mariner we draw back. Part of the cost is the truth of seeing ourselves as we really are, hopeless sinners in need of a Savior. We must come to God on His terms believing that the Master Mariner came to save sinners.

> *"None is righteous, no, not one; no one under-stands; no one seeks for God. All have turned aside; together they have become worthless; no one does good, not even one."* (Rom. 3:10-12)

> *"For all have sinned and fall short of the glory of God."* (Rom. 3:23)

All men must recognize that unless you're a sinner you don't need a Savior. It is so easy to falsely judge ourselves by comparing ourselves to others and their sins and saying to ourselves "I don't look so bad" or "I'm better than they are." All mankind is lost in the sea of life; the Chart Book tells us that we are all are corrupt, evil, and not capable of good without some self-interest. The Chart Book tells the story of a prostitute that the Lord our Master Mariner met at a well. He had the spirit of truth and was a mirror to her and told her all about her sins. She received the truth and saw her sin, and placed her hope in Him. He explained to her *"Those that worship Him must worship in spirit and in truth."* (John 4:24). Men don't want to hear the truth about themselves because they believe that there's something good in every person, particularly themselves. We believe we can worship the Master Mariner without walking in truth. We need to be confronted with the hopelessness of our sin nature in order to walk in truth. The very essence of truth is that man was born with a corrupt sin nature and his condition is hopeless without the redeeming grace of God.

After many days of storms, we are thrust by big waves over coral reefs into a quiet harbor. We barely made it over these reefs. I heard the keel of the ship grind on the coral as we passed over the last reef into a beautiful large harbor. I'm sure we would not have made it if the captain had not told us to throw all our personal effects overboard including our clothes and everything we owned. Clothes speak of the profession and status in life. Some of the brothers had rich clothing and some had tattered rags as clothes. Everything had to be left behind. We were naked for just a moment and after we entered the harbor, we were covered with white gowns like a wedding garment prepared for a King. The top of the gown around the neckline was sprinkled with drops of blood and under the neck was written the *Righteousness of Christ.* No man could go ashore or hope eventually to appear later before the King at the wedding of His bride in Heaven without wearing the wedding garment. Yet many men try, clothed in their own righteousness, and eventually will be cast into outer darkness. (Matt. 22:1-14)

I didn't know what to expect when we arrived. I thought the Promised Land was going to be like Heaven. I asked the crew who told me that this was a type of the Kingdom of God where there were still enemies to conquer and also blessings on the way over the mountains to eventually arrive in Paradise and see the King. We had gone through the seas of tribulation not unlike the Israelites who spent forty years in the desert, and now new enemies to conquer.

The sun came out and we saw that we had arrived to the Promised Land. The land was very mountainous and had a large mesa, or flat-topped mountain, in the center of what appeared to be a Peninsula. There was a large bay to the north with a wide opening and there were many masts sticking through the water as evidence of shipwrecks. None of the large ships could cross the shallow reefs to reach the main part of the land where we landed. Our crew anchored in the harbor and then took on fresh supplies. There were abundant fruit trees and fresh water, And the climate was perfect. The beaches were pristine and as white as snow. The water was warm and contained a great many fish. It seemed as if we'd arrived in Paradise. The captain of the ship and many of the crew stayed on the ship and after being resupplied turned the ship around and went back over the reef to the wide stormy oceans to gather more citizens of heaven and bring them home. As I looked out to sea, I saw several more sailing ships following us. They were of different sizes in different colors and no two ships were exactly alike. UŨ Some of the ships were named Prudence, Righteousness, Obedience, Chastity, Tenacity, Grace, Hospitality, Faith, Goodness, Graciousness, and Evangel. Many ships had foreign appearing crewmen with different skin colors who spoke languages that I didn't understand but they were all very excited at arriving at the Promised Land. It was interesting to note that only sailing ships driven by the wind of the spirit made it to the safe harbor. The motor driven ships and larger ships all headed north to a broad entrance that appeared to be a large harbor. Others told me that the water in the North passage was broad and deep but quickly narrowed and many ships were lost after hitting rocky shoals. Several motor driven ships had tried across the shallow reefs unsuccessfully and their hulls littered the beach. Some of the names of the ships littering the beach were Enlightenment, Human Wisdom, Modern Thinking, Broad Mindedness, Scientific Revolution, Freedom, Revolution, Evolution, Pragmatism, Tolerance, Self-Discovery, Easy Believism, Prosperity, and many other isms. yielding to

God's plan for their lives. When we look at the cost of losing all to gain the Master Mariner we draw back. Part of the cost is the truth of seeing ourselves as we really are, hopeless sinners in need of a Savior. We must come to God on His terms believing that the Master Mariner came to save sinners.

> *"None is righteous, no, not one; no one under-stands; no one seeks for God. All have turned aside; together they have become worthless; no one does good, not even one."* (Rom. 3:10-12)

> *"For all have sinned and fall short of the glory of God."* (Rom. 3:23)

All men must recognize that unless you're a sinner you don't need a Savior. It is so easy to falsely judge ourselves by comparing ourselves to others and their sins and saying to ourselves "I don't look so bad" or "I'm better than they are." All mankind is lost in the sea of life; the Chart Book tells us that we are all are corrupt, evil, and not capable of good without some self-interest. The Chart Book tells the story of a prostitute that the Lord our Master Mariner met at a well. He had the spirit of truth and was a mirror to her and told her all about her sins. She received the truth and saw her sin and placed her hope in Him. He explained to her *"Those that wor-ship Him must worship in spirit and in truth."* (John 4:24). Men don't want to hear the truth about themselves because they believe that there's something good in every person, particularly themselves. We believe we can worship the Master Mariner without walking in truth. We need to be confronted with the hopelessness of our sin nature to walk in truth. The very essence of truth is that man was born with a corrupt sin nature and his condition is hopeless without the redeeming grace of God.

Chapter 20

BROAD IS THE WAY

There were little huts along the beach and very friendly people greeted us. The land was beautiful, a land literally flowing with milk and honey. They had decided not to go any further even though one could tell that heaven was on the other side of the mountains. They were like the tribes of Reuben, Gad, and half tribe of Manasseh who preferred the peace and safety of the east side of the Jordan. They said they felt so comfortable and were so blessed to be in such a beautiful place that they decided to go no further. About a half-mile behind the beach and coconut palms was a series of cliffs that made it difficult to cross the peninsula. There was a path that led up the mountain called *"The Difficult Way."* There was another path which was very well kept up and wide and paved called *"The Broad and Easy Way"* that led north toward the broad bay and circumnavigated the mountains and avoided the difficulties of climbing over the mountains. It was lined with resting places, nice restaurants, playing fields, and shade from the sun.

I asked the local people about the enemies of God that needed to be conquered in the Promised Land. They were called pride, lust, greed, arrogance, envy, divisiveness, idolatry, anger, selfish ambitions, heresies, drunkenness, adultery, doubt, fear, laziness, apathy, sloth, gluttony, and sorcery. Many of the enemies were very large and powerful and were as giants in the land. These giants ate people and liked to live near the Broad and Easy Way where they could sneak up on people who were resting in the shady places! The local beach people hoped to avoid them rather than confront and conquer them. They had hoped that once in the Promised Land, life would be easy.

Meanwhile, the people on the beach divided into three groups. One group had decided to stay on the beach and another group had decided to take the Broad Way through the Broad Gate toward heaven. The third group had decided to take the Difficult Way and the narrow path. There were only a few others who decided to climb this difficult tortuous path with me. I rejoice that I had company. We were all aware of the potential attacks by the enemy. We knew we had to overcome our fear and doubt as we climbed this mountain path. We recognized we were vulnerable to fits of anger and selfish ambitions. I knew I had to conquer my competitive spirit that always wanted to be first. I knew I had to let others go before me and watch out over the weak.

Our small group huddled in prayer and asked God for grace to make this dangerous journey up the mountainside. We understood the forthcoming trials of our flesh would help us learn to trust Christ and make Him alone our hope. It seems that men always have some hope in themselves and when man hopes entirely in Christ, it is only for a moment and usually because of a crisis. He then falls back to his old ways and his own self-sufficiency. Persevering hope comes through trials, the testimonies of others, reading His Word, and fellowship with our Lord.

The path of *"The Difficult Way"* was so narrow that only one person at a time could walk on it. It was very slippery when wet and muddy, and many fell but most picked themselves up and went on. Waterfalls and streams crossed it as it went up the mountain. There were many thorn bushes and poisonous plants such as poison ivy along this narrow path. The tropical foliage was so thick that it could easily hide an attacking enemy. The trees were so large that they often blocked the sunlight. I felt intense depression and discouragement when traversing parts of the path where there was no sunlight.

The path seemed to be carved by others out of the side of the mountain. In some steep rocky areas, there were steps hewn out the rock. The path I was following was very old and there were deep impressions in the rock from footprints indicating extensive wear in the past. It did not appear to have been used much recently. There were many newer paths up the mountain that seemed much better, safer, and well used. Many broke away from our group to follow the newer paths, but some of us continued on the ancient paths even though they appeared to be much more difficult and dangerous.

> *"But my people have forgotten me; they make offerings to false gods; they made them stumble in their ways, in the ancient roads, and to walk into side roads, not the highway."* (Jer. 18:15)

For some strange reason I had felt compelled to climb up the mountain. At times I felt foolish because I had fallen many times and was scratched, bruised, and hungry. I often wondered if I had taken the right path. It was the encouragement of my fellow travelers that helped me to press forward. They gave me vision for the joy of reaching the top of the mountain where I could look eastward and see heaven itself.

As we began the climb up the mountainside there were complaints about the pain, suffering, and about bleeding feet and scratches by thorns. We could feel the comfort of the prayers of saints and it was comforting to know that others had gone before us. As we climbed the mountainside knowing that *"tribulations produce perseverance and perseverance, proven character, and proven character hope, a hope that does not disappoint."* (**Rom. 5:3-5**) In our trials we saw the wisdom of God in tribulation. We began to see there was no easy way to avoid the crucified life.

As the paths up the mountain leveled out, some wanted to take a break to sit down and rest, and some talked about turning back. We encouraged one another to press on and that encouragement by fellow travelers was so meaningful. We knew within ourselves that we were weak and that we needed each other. The love of the Lord began to flow between one another as we appreciated each other's strengths and at the same time loved people in spite of their weaknesses. The demons of doubt were full of anger and they mocked and tormented us with questions. These were questions we'd heard before. How could a good God or God of love create such misery? They told us that we were going nowhere and what we believed was a dead end. They also told us that we were lost and on the wrong path; that there was another path called the Easy Way up the mountain and that we were on the ancient Difficult Way and few would make it.

These mockers and tormentors became more severe and frequent when the highway dropped into a small valley. They had rested there and when we came through they laughed at us and called us foolish. We were poor and hungry and our gowns were tattered and torn so that we were nearly naked. We comforted one another and thought this was the most painful part of the trip. We could endure physical pain but the rejection of men was much more painful. A few of our group became angry and turned against the Lord and all of us and again said we were going nowhere, and it was a useless journey, and they decided that they were going to take the Easy Way. This broke our hearts. They took their frustration out on us by beating us with sticks.

I must confess that at the time I also felt like turning back, but the love of God drew me on. The Holy Spirit comforted us throughout the immeasurable difficulty of the trip. It was very painful to see family and friends on the shore when we arrived at the island. They urged us to turn to the easy way. They rebuked us for choosing the difficult way. We had no money for supplies, food, or water. We picked berries and found some fruit along the way. There were many streams with clear mountain water. We knew that God would supply our needs. As we got higher up the mountainside, we could look around the island.

After coming around a bend on the trail, a vista and viewing point opened up to us. Below there were golf courses, playgrounds, tennis courts, football fields and all kinds of other sports fields. It appeared that there were many great restaurants. We could see their neon signs along the broad way. We felt miserable and hungry for good food. Again we questioned ourselves and wondered if we made a great mistake. Being able to see the pleasure of others, particularly those eating outside in lovely restaurants, seemed to increase our pain when we compared our plight with theirs. We could hear the laughter in music as people celebrated and rejoiced as they went on the *"The Easy Way."* My heart mourned at the Satanic delusion these people were under. I could see that the spirits of pride, lust, self-sufficiency, envy, arrogance, selfish ambitions, heresies, and a variety of other besetting sins were attacking them.

We had to remind each other that the way of the Lord is often painful but our reward would be in heaven, not on earth. We had to learn to be grateful for what little food and water that we did have, and in all things thank God for the good and bad.

> *"Giving thanks always and for everything to God the Father in the name of our Lord Jesus Christ."* (Eph. 5:20) *"I will offer to you the sacrifice of thanksgiving and call on the name of the Lord."* (Ps. 116:17) *"Pray without ceasing, give thanks in all circumstances; for this is the will of God in Christ Jesus for you."* (1 Thess. 5:17-18)

I remembered the Scripture from the Chart Book, which said "all those that desire to live a godly life in Christ Jesus will be persecuted, while evil people and imposters go from good to worse deceiving and being deceived,"(2 Tim. 3:12-13). I remember when Jesus said to his disciples, *"if anyone desires to come after me let him deny himself and take up his cross and follow* me. *For whoever desires to save his life will lose it, but whoever loses his life for my sake will save it, for with what profit is it to a man if he gains the whole world and loses his own soul? Or what will a man give up in exchange for his soul?"* (Mark 8:34-36)

As I meditated on the Scriptures from the Chart Book, the Lord reminded me that the only good Christian is a dead Christian! The only trustworthy man is a man who's died to himself and his selfish ambitions. A dead man doesn't complain to the Lord and doesn't demand anything or special treatment since he is dead. A dead man has freedom from the attachments of the world, but he can say, "Lord it's all about You and You alone and You desire perfect obedience." The apostle Paul said, "*I die daily.*" I too must die each day to my own desires and say, "Have Your way with me Lord." Then I meditated on the things that happened to me: how I had started on a cruise ship along the way, became ship wrecked, and I lost my money, my job, my family, my social status, my reputation, my friends, my health, and my clothes when I came to the Promised Land. I was a sorry sight indeed. I new I couldn't go back. I must die to the things in my past that had kept me captive to this world and move on. Oh how I struggled! It was the fellowship of the other saints on the same path that encouraged me and I them. We knew that the enemy could easily attack us and make us fall if he could isolate us. Oh, how we needed each other.

Chapter 21

FALSE AND TRUE FINISHES

The further we traveled on the trail the more difficult it became. The trail's name changed to the *Trail of Difficulty* and I knew that I couldn't have made it if others hadn't gone before us to blaze the way. We finally clawed our way to the top of the flat top mountain. We couldn't believe our eyes, which gleamed when we saw the beauty of the mountaintop. There was a large lake in the center with crystal-clear water and the lake was said to be very deep. The surrounding area was beautiful and filled with many fruit trees and lovely thick grass. There were many steam baths and the lake water was warm. This kept the climate in this beautiful bowl very mild even though we were several thousand feet above the sea below. As we walked along the edge of the mountain top we could use the entire island. To the North was the Broad Way, which led around a beautiful bay. There were many shipwrecks along the shores of the bay. To the East was Paradise. We could see the glow of the light of Christ the King, in many beautiful colors. Even at night there was light coming from the East that never stopped. To the South was more land and mountains, and of course, to the West was the sea.

We met many other travelers who had settled down in this beautiful place. I asked one of them what the name of this beautiful place was and he answered, *We Have Arrived*. I thought that was a strange name for a place this beautiful but I began to understand that these sojourners were so happy to find respite at the end of this most difficult path that they decided to relax and stay. This was like a combination of Eden and Paradise to them! They knew eventually they would have to move on but that could wait till later and they were happy just to enjoy the beauty of the place and the wonderful fruit and of course, they could take unlimited hot baths in the steam baths that surrounded the lake.

The Holy Spirit prompted me to look with open eyes at the mountaintop. I noticed that the waters were unseasonably warm and very clear. I noted the edge all around the mountaintop was significantly higher than the lake and realized that this was an ancient extinct volcano. The steam vents meant that there was still some activity deep down in the earth.

Again, from the top of this mountain, I looked east into the true Paradise and the deep valley, which separated me from Paradise. The east side of the mountain was in the rain shadow and received very little rain. It was very rocky and had mostly desert vegetation with many thorn bushes. It seemed so ironic that I had to descend the mountain into a deep valley after my struggles to get to the top of this mountain. I immediately understood why many others wanted to stay on the mountaintop.

On the far side of the Mesa facing east was a very narrow trail down a barren and rocky mountainside towards Paradise itself. The trail appeared to be very tortuous and had many switchbacks as it went back and forth down the mountainside but then disappeared into a stand of trees at the base of the mountain. Then it was no longer visible. We travelers thoroughly enjoyed our experience from the mountaintop, but something was nagging at me to leave the others and go on. I began to see that in the journey towards God, that there were many false finishes to the race. Some of my fellow travelers had been through so much difficulty that they felt they deserved to be on the mountaintop and didn't need to go on any further or down into the valley. They had avoided the valley and *"The Easy*

Way." They felt they had earned this respite from the troubles of this world. After all, they had done so much for our Lord; and hadn't they sacrificed so much to get to the mountaintop? Surely God must be pleased with them. Yet I was looking for more, a place to serve as well as to worship my Lord. I was not seeking a place of eternal rest and comfort.

I met many famous and war weary Christians at the mountaintop who felt too tired to press on. The way down the east side of the mountain was very steep and treacherous. Many of these saints felt that Jesus would come and get them and bring them into heaven or paradise when He was ready.

With great difficulty I chose to move on and leave this beautiful paradise. I descended the mountain slowly toward the true Paradise and reached a very dense forest at the bottom of the valley surrounding a beautiful small river. I was cut and bruised from many falls and scratched and bleeding from thorn bushes. The trees were beautiful and large and surrounded a thick wall on the other side of the river that was more than fifty feet high and at least twenty feet thick. I immersed myself in the clear clean water of the river, washed and swam to the other side. Once I arrived at the other side of the river, I saw that the wall extended completely around Paradise itself and separated it from the Promised Land. Many of us had thought that once we entered the Promised Land that we could simply cross over the mountains and enter Paradise. We didn't see the Promised Land as a place of testing and much difficulty. We thought we had finally arrived in a place of prosperity and rest.

I didn't expect such an impenetrable large, thick, and tall wall. I thought I could just walk into Paradise. I saw no doors in the wall at first. Finally, I came to a large glass vessel set up as a shower. It looked like it contained blood. I stood underneath it and pulled the ring and realized I had been washed again in the blood of Christ. I stepped out of the shower and my clothes were snow white and all my wounds had been healed. Nearby I saw a small door measuring about fifteen inches high and twenty-four inches wide, just big enough for a small child. I opened the door and on the other side through a long tunnel I could see the glory of the Lord, which was unbelievably beautiful. The beauty was beyond description and took my breath away momentarily. The light was very intense like a laser that had the potential to destroy had I not been clothed in the gown of the Righteousness of Christ and washed in His blood.

I realized that there was no way I could squeeze through such a small door. I was extremely excited just to see God's glory and I was so thankful that I was even able to open the small door. I felt a burden to praise the Lord and I bowed down with thanksgiving and began to praise him. I realized how unworthy I was to have gotten to this holy place. I realized that it was not by works that I had done it but entirely by God's grace! I praised and worshiped the Lord for a long period of time and then looked up and I saw the door appeared to be larger or I was smaller. Initially. I couldn't be sure whether I had gotten smaller, or the door was larger. However, as I looked at my surroundings, I realized I had gotten much smaller as I humbled myself and worshiped the Lord. I was now able to climb into the tunnel that was on the other side of the door. Immediately, a warm wind sucked me through the tunnel to the other side, to Paradise itself. I felt so unworthy because I knew I had been saved by grace alone and not by any good works and that all glory belonged to God. I worshipped again and fell on my knees and thanked the Lord that He did it all. I was so unworthy, yet this sojourner was *Home at Last*. I knew that my new home was temporary where I would await my new assignment in the Lord's work and forever serve my eternal King.

> *"And calling to him a child, He put him in the midst of them and said, "Truly, I say to you, unless you turn and become like children, you will never enter the kingdom of heaven. Whoever humbles himself like this child is the greatest in the kingdom of heaven." (Matt.18:2-4)*

Later, I felt a violent shaking, and from location in Paradise I looked back to the mountain from which I came and saw that what seemed to be a Holy mountain was now an active volcano. Fire and lava spued from the top and what were once such a beautiful lake!

Chapter 22

FEAR GOD

EPILOGUE

Just after I passed through the wall, I noted the earth shaking. Eventually I saw smoke coming from the mountaintop and the dormant volcano began to erupt. The great earth quaking was sure to start a tidal wave and those that rested along the shore would be swept away. I knew that all heaven weeps for the lost but at the same time God's judgments are sure. *"Broad is the way that leads to destruction and narrow is the way that leads to life and only a few will find it."* (Matt. 7:13-14) Many who reach the Promised Land or enter the Kingdom of God are excited about God, but never learn His ways. They are more interested in the "milk and honey" of the Promised Land than the Lord of the land. They assume that once they have entered the race, they will finish it. They seem unaware of the many who trip and fall and never complete the race. Some churches teach, "once saved always saved" or eternal security. I certainly believe that those chosen by God before the foundation of this world to be His children will be saved and none will be lost. (Ephesians 1:4-14) However, many of us think we are saved, and we are not! In the United States of America surveys have suggested that less than one out of ten people claiming to be born again Christians actually have a living, saving faith. God will never lose any of His children (John 6:37, 10:27-30), but there are a great many who have false assurance and will be lost. Each believer needs to be periodically challenged to re-evaluate his relationship with God. Pastors, led by compassion, often try to encourage believers with assurance of salvation while the great men of the past such as George Whitfield and Jonathan Edwards emphasized mankind's self-deception and lack of true repentance and regeneration. These men emphasized the wrath of God and certainty of eternal damnation in Hell; a message heard too infrequently today. We are all human and hence very vulnerable to self-deception. *The heart is deceitful above all things and desperately wicked. Who can know it?* (Jer. 17:9) It is the trials, troubles, and tribulations of life that help us see our true position and ourselves with our Lord. I often think of John's disappointment with members of his own church when he said: *"They went out from us, but they were not of us; for if they had been of us, they would have continued with us. But they went out, that it might become plain that they all are not of us."*(1 John 2:19) Even apostle John with all of his discernment and anointing had church members that were presumably saved or converted until there was a moment of accountability and they left the fellowship.

There are many false finishes along the racecourse of life. When man gets comfortable and has his needs met, he thinks he has God's approval. He then gets comfortable with his position with God and puts his feet up and rests from the race. Those men on the beach and on the mountaintop in this story had lost their fear of God!

What do I mean by "they have lost their fear of God?" Those that fear God know Him as their loving Father, who also is to be feared and will discipline His children. If you are not disciplined it is because you are not His child.

> *"If you endure chastening, God deals with you as with sons; for what son is there whom a father does not chasten? But if you are without chastening, of which all have become partakers, then you*

are illegitimate and not sons. Furthermore, we have had human fathers who corrected us, and we paid them respect. Shall we not much more readily be in subjection to the Father of spirits and live? For they indeed for a few days chastened us as seemed best to them, but He for our profit, that we may be partakers of His holiness. Now no chastening seems to be joyful for the present, but painful; nevertheless, afterward it yields the peaceable fruit of righteousness to those who have been trained by it." (Heb. 12:5-11)

With all his wisdom, Solomon repeatedly speaks of the fear of the Lord in the Book of Proverbs beginning with:

Proverbs 1:7 *"The fear of the Lord is the beginning of knowledge."*

Proverbs 1:28 *"Then they will call upon me, but I will not answer; they will seek me diligently but will not find me. Because they hated knowledge and did not choose the fear of the Lord."*

Proverbs 2:5 *"Then you will understand the fear of the Lord and find the knowledge of God."*

Proverbs 3:7 *"Be not wise in your own eyes; fear the Lord, and turn away from evil. It will be healing to your flesh and refreshment to your bones."*

Proverbs 8:13 *"The fear of the Lord is hatred of evil. Pride and arrogance and the way of evil and perverted speech I hate."*

If the "fear of the Lord" is to hate evil, then this fear must lead to personal holiness and hatred of all those things that are unclean before the Lord.

Proverbs 9:10 *"The fear of the Lord is the beginning of wisdom, and the knowledge of the Holy One is insight."*

Proverbs 10:27 *"The fear of the Lord prolongs life, but the years of the wicked will be short."*

Proverbs 14:26-27 *"In the fear of the Lord one has strong confidence, and his children will have a refuge. The fear of the Lord is a fountain of life, that one may turn away from the snares of death."*

Proverbs 15:16 *"Better is a little with the fear of the Lord than great treasure and trouble with it."*

Proverbs 15:33 *"The fear of the Lord is instruction in wisdom, and humility comes before honor."*

Proverbs 19:23 *"The fear of the Lord leads to life and whoever has it rests satisfied; he will not be visited by harm."*

Proverbs 22:4 *"The reward for humility and fear of the Lord is riches and honor and life."*

Proverbs 24:21 *"My son, fear the Lord and the king, and do not join with those who do otherwise, for disaster will arise suddenly from them, and who knows the ruin that will come from them both?"*

Proverbs 28:14 *"Blessed is the one who fears the Lord always, but whoever hardens his heart will fall into calamity."*

> Proverbs 31:30 Charm *is deceitful, and beauty is vain, but a woman who fears the Lord is to be praised.*

Finally, at the end of the Book of Ecclesiastes, Solomon concludes his teaching and advises with:

> *"The end of the matter; all has been heard.* <u>*Fear God and keep his commandments, for this is the whole duty of man*</u>. *For God will bring every deed into judgment, with every secret thing, whether good or evil."* (Eccles. 12:13)

The Hebrew word *Yare* or fear is translated as "fear" 188 times, "afraid" 78 times, "terrible" 23 times, "terrible thing" 6 times, "dreadful" 5 times, "reverence" 3 times, "fearful" 2, and the word fear is used for a total of 314 times in the AV or King James Version. The twentieth century church usually downplays the word fear and substitutes the word reverence, which is a much weaker word. People revere their favorite sports figure or movie star. The concept of being afraid of God conflicts with the modern understanding of God as a loving, non-judgmental, feminine mother God. God is very masculine. He tells us that He is a jealous God, full of wrath against the wicked. He is coming to judge and destroy this world by fire. The wicked face eternal judgment in Hell. He is to be feared!!

The fear of the Lord is to *Hate Evil,* yet modern man can't understand how a loving God can hate evil! This is because we don't understand God's holiness. A holy God hates or loathes that which is unholy. We think that God doesn't see our own personal sin and the evil of this fallen world. If we are to have fellowship with God, we must learn to see the world as He sees it. We are not to hate our fellow man but to hate sin and corruption as God does.

It was the fear of the Lord that caused men to cry out at Pentecost: *"Men and brethren what shall we do?"* (Acts 2:37) and

205

the Philippian jailer to cry: *"Sirs, what must I do to be saved?"* (Acts 16:30)

I can remember misbehaving as a small boy and my mother warning me, that if I didn't stop misbehaving, she would tell my father when he got home about my bad behavior. I loved and respected my father and didn't want to disappoint him, so I was careful not to offend him and I did what was necessary to please him. My father never abused me but was a large man who would rarely exhibit righteous anger. To me the whole world shook when he was angry. I had more than reverence for my father. I had genuine fear, particularly when I deserved a spanking. I was just like Adam, who had intimate fellowship with Father God. After Adam sinned in the Garden of Eden, he said: *"I was afraid, because I was naked, and I hid myself* "(Gen. 3:10). If there was any man created by God who had a very intimate love relationship with God, it was Adam. Yet Adam feared God because he knew that his Father was a God of Justice and Holiness who demanded righteousness. Adam knew that God would exact severe consequences for disobedience to His spoken word.

I knew that my father loved me, as did Adam, and could never reject me as his son. If we love God, we want to please Him and therefore we try our best to obey Him. The fear of God is more than being afraid of displeasing our heavenly Father because we love Him. It is also about knowing that sin has painful consequences! God should be feared because He is Holy and Righteous and will punish sin. We should tremble at His Word.

Hebrews 10:30-31 *"Vengeance is mine; I will repay."* And again, *"The Lord will judge his people."* It is a fearful thing to fall into the hands of the living God."

Hebrews 12:28-29 *"let us offer to God acceptable worship, with reverence and awe (or fear), for our God is a consuming fire."*

Notice that reverence and fear or awe are separated and not inclusive. Some define the fear of the Lord as only reverence and do not include the word fear because they do not have a Holy dread, awe, or fear of God. If we ignore the truth of God's wrath, we compromise the gospel message. If God is not full of just wrath, then there is no need for the cross, nor fear of the judgment to come or fear of eternal punishment. **The Holy Wrath of a Just God is central to the gospel message.** The holy wrath of a just God is a missing message in the church today. Jesus came to satisfy the wrath of God. It is His righteousness that protects us from the eternal punishment that we all deserve. If God is a loving God and not a God of wrath, then there is no reason to fear or obey God. Jesus would have died in vain if man is basically good and loved by God and man will not face eternal punishment! The Gospel begins with the fall of man and God's wrath at man's sin. God sent his son to be the propitiation for our sin since no man is righteous. ("...*flesh and blood cannot inherit the kingdom of God; nor does corruption inherit incorruption.*") Jesus fulfilled God's demand for perfect righteousness and thus satisfied His wrath. (*The first Adam became a living being and the second Adam a life-giving spirit.*) Jesus was crucified and arose triumphantly on the third day having purchased for His elect resurrection life now and forever. "*Jesus will reign until He has put all enemies under His foot. The last enemy to be destroyed is death.*" (1 Corinthians 15: 20-26,45,50)

Paul concludes First Corinthians fifteen with words of encouragement. **If we fear God, we not fear death.**

> "*For the trumpet will sound, and the dead will be raised imperishable, and we shall be changed. For this perishable body must put on the imperishable, and this mortal body must put on immortality. When the perishable puts on the imperishable, and the mortal puts on immortality, then shall come to pass the saying that is written:*
>
> "*Death is swallowed up in victory.*" "*O death, where is your victory? O death, where is your sting?*"

The sting of death is sin, and the power of sin is the law. But thanks be to God, who gives us the victory through our Lord Jesus Christ.

Therefore, my beloved brothers, be steadfast, immovable, always abounding in the work of the Lord, knowing that in the Lord your labor is not in vain." (1 Corinthians 15:52-58)

The fear of God is a gift of God. Jeremiah 32:40 says: *"I will put My fear in their hearts, that they shall not depart from me,"* and 32:39, *"Then I will give them one heart and one way that they may fear me forever for the good of them and their children after them."* It is one of God's treasures, Isaiah 33:6 says: *"The fear of the*

Lord is His treasure." We need to all pray for more of that treasure, the Holy fear of the Lord."

Isaiah 66:2 says: *"But on this one I will look on him who is poor and of a contrite spirit, and who trembles at my word".* Verse 5 repeats the same admonition to give it more emphasis: *"Hear the word of the Lord, **you who tremble at His word."***

Fear God, wait for the Lord. *"For the Lord spoke thus to me with his strong hand upon me and warned me not to walk in the way of this people, saying: **"Do not call conspiracy all that this people calls conspiracy, and do not fear what they fear, nor be in dread. But the Lord of hosts, him you shall honor as holy. Let him be your fear and let him be your dread.** And he will become a sanctuary and a stone of offense and a rock of stumbling to both houses of Israel, a trap, and a snare to the inhabitants of Jerusalem. And many shall stumble on it. They shall fall and be broken; they shall be snared and taken."* (Isa. 8:11-15)

We live in a time of great fear about the future and there is much talk about various conspiracy plans amongst world leaders. God is in control, and we are not to live in fear of what man can do, but to fear God and we will have perfect peace and not stumble. **Finally, *"the fear of the Lord"* means obedience!** Abraham waited until he was 100 years old to have a son. His hope for future generations was upon Isaac, but suddenly God spoke to Abraham and said, *"Take your son, your only son Isaac, whom you love, and go to the land of Moriah, and offer him there as a burnt* offering on one of the mountains of which I shall tell you," (Gen. 22:2). Abraham obeyed and told his servants, *"Stay here with the donkey; I and the boy will go over there and worship and come again to you,"* (Gen. 22:5, this is the first mention of worship in the Bible and is an example of obedience and the fear of God.)

Abraham obeyed God and placed Isaac on the altar and was prepared to kill him when God spoke again and said, *"Do not lay your hand on the boy or do anything to him, for **now I know that you fear God**, seeing you have not withheld your son, your only son, from me...* and in your offspring shall all the nations of the earth be blessed, **because you have obeyed my voice,"** (Gen. 22:12&18).

What we men often worship is that which is more important to us than God Himself, such as our dreams, homes, jobs, position, sports, physical fitness, health, wealth, loved ones, beauty, friendships, children, etc. To know God and to fear Him is to obey Him and place everything we love on the altar. **What we withhold from God is that which we worship and that is what defines our relationship with God!** Worship or *worthship* is proportional to the value we place on God above everything else. (Rom. 12:1) It is also proportional to our obedience to Him. (John 14:15) True worship is extravagant focused love and adoration, based on who He is and what He has done for us, displayed by extreme submission, humility, and obedience.

"I appeal to you therefore, brothers, by the mercies of God, to present your bodies as a living sacrifice, holy and acceptable to God, which is your spiritual worship. Do not be conformed to this world but be transformed by the renewal of your mind, that by testing you may discern what is the will of God, what is good and acceptable and perfect." (Rom. 12:1-2)

It is this fear of God that encourages us to press on through difficulties and not get complacent. It is this desire to please and obey Him, that will get us *Home at Last!*

CONCLUSION

At the conclusion of this book, I now return to my professional role as a practicing physician. I have been asked to give my best assessment of what the final diagnosis of the American Church is! There are still some fine healthy churches in America remaining, which have not fallen ill. There are many more that have been infected but are not aware of their illness. I have carefully listed many of the symptoms of this fatal illness, including greed, lust, covetousness, selfishness, self-righteousness, pride, arrogance, lack of humility, narcissism, deception, and a religious spirit. I have performed a careful examination of the patient and performed appropriate testing. My conclusion is that this is a severe, near fatal, case of national narcissism or *"Self Pox!"* We live in the age of entitlement. This is due to the independent, proud, self-confident, self-reliant, self-focused, narcissistic American Spirit. It is a fatal illness if not treated! The treatment is often very painful, and many have suffered for decades with frequent relapses. The treatment is self-evaluation followed by humility, faith, confession, and repentance. This illness is highly contagious and is epidemic in America. It has already been spread to too much of the world. It is too late to be quarantined. Fortunately, there is a vaccine available. It is the Cross of Christ! We have all eaten of the poisoned fruit of "the tree of knowledge of good and evil." **There is a divine antidote, and it is the blood and cross of Jesus acquired only through humility and repentance.** Those who return and who are humbled, cling to the message of the cross, repent, and fear God will be protected form this insidious illness. Perhaps then, the Lord will show mercy and bring revival to America. (Eph 4:22-24)